UNDER
THE
INFLUENCE
OF JESUS

Other Books by Joe Paprocki

The Catechist's Toolbox: How to Thrive as a Religious Education Teacher

La caja de herramientas del catequista: cómo triunfar en el ministerio de la catequesis

Beyond the Catechist's Toolbox: Catechesis That Not Only Informs but Also Transforms

Más allá de la caja de herramientas del catequista: catequesis que no solo informa, sino que también transforma

The Bible Blueprint: A Catholic's Guide to Understanding and Embracing God's Word

Los planos de la Biblia: una guía católica para entender y acoger la Palabra de Dios

Living the Mass: How One Hour a Week Can Change Your Life (with Fr. Dominic Grassi)

Vivir la misa: cómo una hora a la semana puede combiar tu vida (con el Padre Dominic Grassi)

Practice Makes Catholic: Moving from a Learned Faith to a Lived Faith

7 Keys to Spiritual Wellness: Enriching Your Faith by Strengthening the Health of Your Soul

A Well-Built Faith: A Catholic's Guide to Knowing and Sharing What We Believe

Una fe bien construida: guía católica para conocer y compartir lo que creemos

UNDER THE INFLUENCE OF JESUS

THE TRANSFORMING EXPERIENCE OF ENCOUNTERING CHRIST

JOE PAPROCKI, DMin

LOYOLAPRESS.
A JESUIT MINISTRY
Chicago

LOYOLA PRESS.
A JESUIT MINISTRY

3441 N. Ashland Avenue
Chicago, Illinois 60657
(800) 621-1008
www.loyolapress.com

Unless otherwise noted, Scripture quotations are from *New Revised Standard Version Bible: Catholic Edition,* copyright © 1989, 1993 National Council of the Churches of Christ in the United States of America. Used by permission. All rights reserved.

Scripture quotation from the *New American Bible, revised edition* © 2010, 1991, 1986, 1970 Confraternity of Christian Doctrine, Washington, D.C., are used by permission of the copyright owner. All Rights Reserved. No part of the *New American Bible* may be reproduced in any form without permission in writing from the copyright owner.

Scripture quotations from the HOLY BIBLE, NEW INTERNATIONAL VERSION® NIV® Copyright © 1973, 1978, 1984, 2011 by Biblica, Inc.® are used by permission. All rights reserved worldwide.

The "NIV" and "New International Version" are trademarks registered in the United States Patent and Trademark Office by Biblica, Inc.® Use of either trademark requires the permission of Biblica, Inc.®

Scripture from the King James Version is indicated by "av."

Cover art credit: ©iStockphoto.com/yai112.

ISBN-13: 978-0-8294-4050-8
ISBN-10: 0-8294-4050-X
Library of Congress Control Number: 2013952510

Printed in the United States of America.

14 15 16 17 18 Bang 10 9 8 7 6 5 4 3 2

To Mike and Amy,

May you always thrive under the influence of the good Lord!

Contents

Introduction

The important question we ask ourselves today is: how can we talk about God in our time? How can we communicate the Gospel so as to open roads to his saving truth in our contemporaries' hearts—that are all too often closed—and minds—that are at times distracted by the many dazzling lights of society? In talking about God . . . we must recover simplicity, we must return to the essence of the proclamation. Speaking of God is communicating what is essential, forcefully and simply, through our words and through our life.
—Pope Benedict XVI

During a recent vacation in Hawaii, my wife and I spent an incredible afternoon at the Polynesian Cultural Center, sampling the cultures of different Polynesian lands—Hawaii, New Zealand, Somoa, and so on. At each "village," we were introduced to the traditions and rituals that have shaped and expressed the way of life for the people of these regions for centuries. What impressed me most was the energy of the ritual expression: it was bold, dramatic, rich, deeply expressive, and highly energizing. I found my imagination stirred, my heart moved, and my senses stimulated as young people performed and explained the ancient rituals of their culture. In short, the expression of their culture and beliefs was *robust.*

As we watched one of the demonstrations, I imagined what it would be like if the next "village" offered a glimpse into the Catholic experience—a visit to the Island of Catholicism. Would people's imaginations be stirred by the demonstration? Would the stories told be dramatic? Would the worship be robust? Would people be drawn into the experience? I then pictured the Mass I had attended the week before at a parish where the music was dull, the prayers were being prayed in a perfunctory manner (by priest and congregation alike), and the homily was so boring that people's eyes were glazing over. I very nearly found myself yelling *Noooooooooooooooo!* as I returned from this nightmarish daydream to the present. My gut reaction was that, in all too many cases, a person viewing the Catholic experience for the first time would not be moved.

And this deeply saddened me. Don't get me wrong. I'm not embarrassed by my Catholic faith. I am, however, often embarrassed by how we are living it and practicing it. Too often, we are just going through the motions.

Now, contrast my nightmare vision with the very first proclamation of the gospel on the birthday of the church: Pentecost. As recorded in Acts of the Apostles, chapter 2, the apostles proclaimed the gospel for the first time on that day. When all was said and done, 3,000 people had been added to the church. That must have been some proclamation!

What accounts for its power? The crowds who gathered to hear the apostles weren't "wowed" by healings or miracles or impressed by soaring rhetoric. Rather, what captured their imagination was the total lack of inhibition displayed by the apostles; so much so that the crowds commented that perhaps these followers of Jesus had been drinking too much wine. And in truth, the apostles *were* preaching while intoxicated—not with "spirits," but with the Holy Spirit. The crowds saw a group of men who should have been terrified to set foot in public taking to the streets filled with uninhibited joy and enthusiasm for Jesus Christ. It was this dramatic and observable transformation in the behavior of a small group of former fishermen and tax collectors that caught the attention of thousands and led them to "sign on" that very day.

In Jesus' time and culture, wine was a staple of daily life—a natural product of an agricultural economy and an ordinary element of meals and social gatherings. Its centrality to everyday life is reflected in Jesus' choice of wine as the material of his first miracle at Cana and as one of the two elements of the Eucharist, as well as in the New Testament authors' use of wine imagery to capture the effects of the Holy Spirit on the mind and heart. While the effects of alcohol can be harmful and even deadly, however, the effects of the Holy Spirit are life giving and transformative. And as both Jesus and the Scripture writers knew, inebriation by the Spirit is what we humans most deeply crave.

In his book *A 12-Step Approach to the Spiritual Exercises of St. Ignatius*, Jim Harbaugh, SJ, explains it this way:

Human beings have wanted for millennia to attain altered states, to expand consciousness, and drugs are one way to do this—a way, as it happens, with too many undesirable side effects, particularly over the long haul. But the principle is sound: we want to be intoxicated in the sense of being able to let go of our niggling little egos, our fears and resentments and narrow-mindedness. We want to have some sense of the great realities around us.

Given this basic human desire for intoxication, it should come as no surprise that one of the most famous traditional prayers of the Catholic Church, the Anima Christi, goes like this: "Soul of Christ, sanctify me; Body of Christ, save me; Blood of Christ, *inebriate me.*" With these words, we pray for the same kind of intoxication—a sober one—that the apostles experienced on the day the church was born.

Somewhere along the way, unfortunately, we lost this robust and ebullient approach to proclaiming the gospel, as if the church had instituted some kind of "prohibition" against the inebriating influence of the Holy Spirit. The goal of this book, *Under the Influence of Jesus: The Transforming Experience of Encountering Christ*, is to send a message, loud and clear, that the time has come for this prohibition to be lifted. The New Evangelization—a renewal and refocusing of the church's mission in the twenty-first century—is a clarion call for Christians all over the world to drink deeply of the Holy Spirit and begin living a transformed life under the influence of Jesus Christ. Being inebriated in this way will not empower us to proclaim the gospel of Jesus Christ through miracles or to mesmerize large crowds with our silver tongues. As it did the apostles on Pentecost, though, it should enable us to demonstrate on an obvious level that the experience of encountering Christ has transformed us into new beings on fire with his message—and that it can likewise transform others.

The powerful mode of preaching that animated the apostles on Pentecost and throughout the period of the early church is known as *kerygma*, a Greek word meaning "proclamation." Whenever the apostles approached a crowd that would be hearing about the risen Christ for the first time, they relied on this type of speech—a simple, basic, Jesus-centered proclamation designed to foster conversion. This is precisely the type of proclamation of the gospel that is urgently needed and indeed required for the New Evangelization.

In this book, we will explore not only what this "kerygmatic" message looks and sounds like, but also the characteristics of the transformed life we are called to live under the influence of Jesus Christ. Such a transformation need not turn us into real-life equivalents of Ned Flanders, the annoyingly perfect, Bible-thumping neighbor of

Homer Simpson. Nor does it turn us into arrogant, self-righteous, and judgmental hypocrites. It *does* turn us into humble, sincere, authentic people who are no longer governed by the worldly powers of pride, fear, anger, lust, or envy, but by "otherworldly" virtues such as charity, joy, peace, patience, kindness, and goodness. This transformation is subtle but observable—just enough to make people wonder what's going on and why. And if they ask, we must "always be ready to make [our] defense to anyone who demands from [us] an accounting for the hope that is in [us]" (1 Peter 3:15).

St. Peter's advice is sound, but we shouldn't always wait to be asked. Knowing Jesus and proclaiming him to others should be simple, direct, compelling, joy-filled, and habitual, and its effects should be life changing. In other words, it should be *kerygmatic* and apostolic. As a church, we are being called to renew our passion for proclamation so as to present Jesus to current and future generations as someone knowable and as someone who can change your life. My hope and prayer is that this book will enable you truly to encounter Christ, embrace his message, and begin living a transformed life under his influence.

There's GOT to Be Another Way!

The Promise of an Alternate Reality

The kingdom of God is at hand.
—Mark 1:15, NAB

In the classic Who song "Who Are You?", we hear about a frustrating day in the life of a rock star who, upon receiving a huge royalty check, celebrated with a drinking binge that nearly landed him in jail. Waking up in a doorway in Soho, he pines, "God, there's GOT to be another way!" Sooner or later, we all come to this point, though the circumstances vary. It happens when we realize that there has to be more to life than what meets the eye. At the heart of Jesus' Good News is the message that there *is* another way. Jesus calls it the kingdom of God—an alternate reality that is in our midst and that promises the fullness of life.

Can't Get No Satisfaction

The Who are not the only now-aging rockers who once put words to a universal feeling of discontent. Mick Jagger of the Rolling Stones famously couldn't "get no satisfaction," for example, and Bruce Springsteen reminded us that "Everybody's got a hungry heart." It's strange, isn't it? We live in the wealthiest nation on earth and in history, and yet we still aren't satisfied. Sometimes this dissatisfaction is acute, taking the form of extreme sadness, depression, or despair. Other times, our dissatisfaction is barely noticeable—more of a gnawing feeling beneath the surface that there should be *more*. But what is that "more" we're looking for?

Simply put, we want to be secure.

To be secure means to be free from danger, free from fear, and free from cares and worries. That's why we play the lottery, escape into the alternate realities of TV, video games, and the Internet, and wrongly use substances like food and alcohol. We long to be in a place or a state where nothing can hurt us and where no obstacle can keep us from our deepest desires. In our quest to find this nirvana, we doggedly pursue the accumulation of wealth, abandon old lives to begin new lives, numb ourselves to our fears and insecurities, or do all three. As in the song "Who Are You?", we find ourselves waking up at some point and exclaiming, "God, there's got to be another way!" We find ourselves coming to the realization that our lives are not what we thought they would be—just like Jerry and George did in an episode of *Seinfeld*. As they sit in the diner after a particularly frustrating day, Jerry begins to question the direction of their lives: "What is this?" he asks. "What are we doing? What in God's name are we doing?" He and George go on to lament their pathetic lives before Jerry resolves, "Well, this is it. I'm really gonna do something about my life, you know? George, I am really gonna make some changes." George agrees and the two shake hands in an apparent commitment to change the course of their lives.

Of course, neither of them turns out to be man enough to make any significant changes in his life. The scene, however, captures the sentiment that most of us feel at one time or another: "God, there's GOT to be another way!" And it's precisely this sentiment that Jesus addresses when he proclaims the central message of his Good News: "The kingdom of God is at hand"! In other words, he's saying, "By God [pun intended], there IS another way!"

Just what is this kingdom of God that Jesus is talking about?

An Alternate Reality

If you've traveled a lot, you know that people talk and act differently in various parts of the country and the world. In Chicago, where I live, you don't go "over to" someone's home; you go "by" their home. Nor do we shop at Kmart or Wal-Mart, but rather at Kmart's and Wal-Mart's. In Pittsburgh, the plural of "you" is sometimes spoken as "yins." In Hawaii, elderly women are referred to as "aunties." In the Middle East, one of the worst insults you can hurl at someone is, literally, your shoe. And in Europe, if you're displeased with your team's play at a sports event, you might whistle instead of booing. Needless to say, if you plan on relocating to a distant region or country, it helps to get to know the language and customs of that place.

But what if your destination is the kingdom of God?

Now, *there's* a strange place! Folks in the kingdom of God speak and act very differently indeed. There, the poor are considered "blest"; enemies are loved; persecutors are prayed for; the exalted are humbled and the humbled, exalted; sins are forgiven (not just seven times but seventy times seven times); feet are washed by the master; and new life is gained through death. Likewise, when folks in this topsy-turvy kingdom speak, their conversations are laced with references to compassion, charity, justice, fortitude, forgiveness, gratitude, patience, kindness, gentleness, and a host of other unlikely concepts. This is indeed an alternate reality! And why do "kingdom-dwellers" act like this? Because they have found security. They are secure in the knowledge that they are not alone and that someone's got their back. And that someone is the Lord of this kingdom, whom they know is in their midst.

Strange as this alternate reality may seem, it's no secret. In fact, the concept of the kingdom of God (also referred to as the "kingdom of heaven" or the "reign of God") is the very heart and soul of Jesus' message. It is what Jesus is all about. It is who Jesus is. If Jesus were running a campaign for public office, his official motto would be "Repent! The kingdom of God is at hand!"—which, according to Mark, was the very first utterance of Jesus' ministry (1:15). Not only was the kingdom of God Jesus' first topic, but it was also one of his most frequent: in the Gospels of Matthew, Mark, and Luke, he refers to it more than eighty times. (In John's Gospel, Jesus opts for the phrase "eternal life"—yet another term for the kingdom—and it appears seventeen times). If you want to know what someone is about, pay attention to what they say and do. In the case of Jesus, his words and actions all point to one thing: an alternate reality he calls the kingdom of God.

Since this kingdom is not a place but a state of being, Jesus is really offering us another way to be human. This other way of being human is grounded in the recognition and acceptance of the reality that, at our deepest level, we are incapable of sustaining ourselves. The invitation to enter the kingdom of God is an invitation to imagine a reality in which God is near and "in charge"—fully present—all the time.

But what does it mean to say that God is "in charge"? It certainly doesn't mean that God wants to boss us around, nor does it mean that we should just sit back and let God figure things out. It doesn't mean that you should skip the treatment a doctor prescribed for a serious illness or go to court without a lawyer because God has "got your back." To say that God is in charge isn't to abdicate our own responsibilities or to ignore the wisdom of our fellow humans, but rather to align our minds, hearts, and wills to his and to place ultimate trust in him—even when, from our limited vantage point, things seem to be going awry. To say that God is in charge is not to say that he is pulling strings and controlling every little detail of our lives. It is simply to say that God's will trumps my will and the will of anyone else. It is to recognize that we are not self-sufficient and that, while we can and must rely on others, our ultimate reliance is on God. It is to imagine and embrace a completely different way of living.

Two Sides of the Same Coin

When it comes to the concept of the kingdom of God, there are two questions we must ask: *What does it say about God?* And *what does it say about us?* Let's start with God. He is the King, after all.

Side 1: What the Kingdom Says about God

The central activity of a king is to *reign*, and a king who reigns effectively is actively present in the kingdom and compels those who live there to follow his will. When Jesus says, "The kingdom of God is at hand," he is saying that God is actively present in this world and in our lives. He is not the distant reality of Enlightenment deism, a "watchmaker" who set creation in motion long ago and then sat back to watch things unfold (with the occasional intervention). The Jews of Jesus' time—living under Roman rule in a Jerusalem that was a shadow of its former self—also felt that God was distant, and they longed for his presence to be felt as it was by their ancestors during the exodus from Egypt. Jesus' bold announcement of the presence of the kingdom of God signaled that God had indeed "returned" to his people and was reigning as their king.

We don't have to wait for a distant God to intervene: in Jesus, God's presence became indelible, impossible to shake off. But then, why would we want to? In their book *King, Warrior, Magician, Lover*, authors Douglas Gillette and Robert Moore help us to see how priceless a true king is. According to Moore and Gillette, the archetypal king

- is centered and centering. The king is the geographic and spiritual center of his realm, bringing order in the midst of chaos.
  His role is to unify.
- is decisive. The king represents firm and unchanging principles,
  and his decisions flow from these principles and are in the best
  interests of his people.
- lives with integrity. His role is to embody integrity and virtue
  and to consistently use these qualities to mend relationships,
  represent truth, and keep his word.
- protects his realm. The king safeguards his realm from danger
  and threats. This includes providing for the needs of the poor
  and vulnerable.
- provides order. The king represents and enforces the law to
  establish order and to ensure that fairness and justice reign.
- creates and inspires creativity in others. The king uses his influence to empower others to achieve their full potential.
- blesses the lives of others. The king recognizes and honors others for their achievements and extends his favor to them.
- leaves a legacy. The king leaves behind a gift to remind future
  generations of his enduring greatness.

Benevolent kings of the past who lived up to these responsibilities were
hailed by their subjects, who eagerly and loyally identified with them.
The same is true of God and of us. When Jesus proclaims that the
kingdom of God is in our midst, he is telling us that God has intervened in our lives to

- bring order to our lives;
- unify his people;

- do what is best for us;
- mend relationships;
- convey the truth;
- fulfill his word;
- protect us from danger;
- provide for order and justice;
- inspire us to live to our full potential;
- affirm us; and
- be with us forever.

And when we see that our God—our King—is like this, we hail him, follow him, and identify with him. He is ours, and we are his. When Jesus taught us to pray "thy kingdom come," he taught us to invite a king who has our best interests in mind to plant his flag in the center of our lives and to do what he does best for our benefit and the benefit of others. To pray the Our Father is to declare that, at our deepest level, we are incapable of sustaining ourselves and therefore happily rely on God, our King. Being his, however, comes with its own set of responsibilities.

Side 2: What the Kingdom Says about Us

And so we flip to the other side of the coin: our role in the alternate reality of the kingdom. Just as the central activity of the king is to *reign*, the central activity of his subjects is to *pledge allegiance*.

This new way of being human—of living in the kingdom of God—begins with the question *To what and to whom do you owe allegiance?* As schoolchildren, we were taught to pledge allegiance to the flag of the United States of America. The citizens of Jesus' time were also required to pledge allegiance to their government, the Roman Empire. Jesus, however, insists that we pledge allegiance to someone and something else. That does not mean that we denounce our nation's flag. It does mean, however, that God's "flag" trumps all other flags. To live in the kingdom of God is to invite God to plant his flag in the center of our lives and to pledge allegiance to it. In doing so, we pledge loyalty and submission to the will of God and to everything that God stands for.

Jesus knew that, in addition to pledging allegiance to ruling governments, we also find ourselves pledging allegiance to many other realities. We pledge allegiance to power, perfection, popularity, pleasure, possessions, and position, for example—and that's just one letter of the alphabet. When we pledge allegiance to any of these worldly realities, our actions flow from them. To *repent*, then, is to shift allegiance. When Jesus calls us to repent, he's not simply asking us to be sorry for a laundry list of momentary lapses in judgment. He's asking us to shift allegiance—to shift our loyalties—as we set foot on a path to citizenship in the kingdom of God. Until we do so, we tend to live like outsiders, hiding in the shadows from the authority of God because our allegiance lies elsewhere.

When we voluntarily pledge allegiance to something, we do so because we believe in what it stands for. We trust that it will protect us and help us to grow toward our full potential. That's why it's so tempting for us to pledge allegiance to wealth, for example. Although our currency has the words "In God We Trust" imprinted on it, let's be honest: we often find ourselves trusting in the power of money over the power of God. We believe that having wealth will protect us and enable us to achieve our goals and reach our full potential. And indeed, money can protect us from many dangers and can smooth the way to achieving some of our goals. The human heart, however, knows that there is more. It refuses to rest until it has pledged allegiance to the one and only thing that can bring true fulfillment: an intimate relationship with our Creator.

What the Kingdom Is NOT

Before we go any further in describing the kingdom of God, let's be sure we are clear about what it is *not*.

The kingdom is not you.

Despite the efforts of various New Age gurus to convince us that the kingdom of God should be equated with our innermost being, the truth is that Jesus never said this. Jesus said that the kingdom of God is "in your midst," meaning "within your grasp." This is sometimes wrongly translated as "the kingdom of God is within." While we are made in the image and likeness of God and are indeed "temples of the Holy Spirit," the kingdom of God is a reality beyond our limited selves. While we can discover a portal to the kingdom within ourselves, if we equate ourselves with the kingdom, we run the risk of becoming mini-tyrants, seeking to impose our will on others. While our minds and hearts belong to the kingdom, it is much vaster and grander than our human minds and hearts can begin to fathom.

The kingdom is not heaven.

Many Christians equate the kingdom of God with the after-life—namely, heaven. Perhaps this is because the Gospels sometimes use the phrase *kingdom of heaven* in place of *kingdom of God*. Even so, it is misleading to think of the kingdom as a reward awaiting us in the afterlife—something we can earn by gritting our teeth and surviving this hell on earth. Jesus' message was not about "later," it was about now. He states in no uncertain terms that the kingdom of God—our ultimate destiny—is a present reality, one that we can participate in now and then fully in the afterlife.

The kingdom is not prosperity.

Some branches of Christianity preach that a sign of the presence of the kingdom of God is prosperity. This is especially true in the United

States, where a proclamation of what can be called the "prosperity gospel" is often heard in the media. Preachers of this ilk claim that prosperity is our birthright and an indication that the kingdom of God is active and present in our lives. It's true that the kingdom of God brings its citizens prosperity, but not financial prosperity. Instead, it brings a surplus—an abundance—of joy, well-being, and love.

The kingdom is not our country.

Patriotic rhetoric often includes religious imagery. American politicians in particular have long invoked the image of the United States as the "city built on a hill" of which Jesus spoke in Matthew 5:14. From Puritan John Winthrop's use of the image to inspire settlers of the Massachusetts Bay Colony, to references in speeches by presidents Kennedy and Reagan, the image of the United States as a shining city of God has given rise to American exceptionalism—the belief that God's kingdom is made manifest on our supposedly sacred shores.

The kingdom is not the church.

Back in the day, before the Second Vatican Council, Catholics did tend to identify the church with the kingdom of God. Who can blame us, though, when popes such as Leo XIII said things like the following: "The kingdom of God on earth [is] the true Church of Jesus Christ." Thankfully, this type of thinking changed with the Second Vatican Council, which spoke of the church as "the seed and the beginning" of the kingdom and explained that, through the church, we learn to long "for the completed kingdom." The church is indeed connected to the kingdom of God and serves it, but it isn't the kingdom itself.

What the Kingdom IS: An Alternate Way

Now that we've pointed out what the kingdom is *not*, let's take a stab at describing more precisely what it *is*. The following image may help.

I've traveled quite a bit, but one of my favorite places to visit is New Orleans. If you've ever been to the French Quarter in that city, you may recall encountering a very peculiar juxtaposition of images. Just as you prepare to enter Bourbon Street, the beautiful Cathedral of St. Louis rises up before your eyes. Around the perimeter of the cathedral are stationed dozens of fortune-tellers, readers, and advisors—and of course, their "clients," people eagerly seeking a glimpse of the ever-veiled future. Meanwhile, Bourbon Street itself is populated with no shortage of businesses eager to fulfill your every desire for pleasure, whether it be in the form of food, drink, music, or sex. While some people find it strange and even unseemly for a cathedral to be situated in such a place, I view the entire scenario as a perfect image of the kingdom of God in our midst. It is a microcosm of life in this world. We are surrounded by people and entities that promise to show us the future and to satisfy us on some or all levels. The experiences that come with these promises are attractive, fun, and alluring, and in fact, we do find gratification in them—temporarily. We also find that we pay the price for some of them the next day!

Indeed, the world offers us myriad ways to gain short-lived satisfaction and to catch a glimpse of what lies ahead. In the midst of all this, however, Jesus proposes an alternate reality—a reality in which we find true and lasting fulfillment and the promise of a God-filled future. Many aspects of the French Quarter are great fun as long as you recognize that they are illusory. The call to live in the kingdom of God is not a call to condemn the entirety of secular living. Rather, it is a call to recognize that, in the midst of what we call the secular world, there lies an alternate reality—a true path to fulfillment that is hard to spot but far from illusory. To answer this call is to repent—literally, to turn and look in a different direction and to train our eyes to perceive this awesome reality.

Slightly Tipsy Behavior

In the introduction to this book, I said that on Pentecost the apostles were intoxicated—that to those who heard them speak, they seemed to be occupying an alternate reality. A few of the people present believed the apostles were, in fact, drunk on wine, and scoffed at them (see Acts 2:13). What else, they wondered, could explain the uninhibited behavior of this small band of men eagerly announcing their allegiance to a convicted criminal who had recently been executed as a traitor to the Roman Empire? But for many others present, the transformation evident in this small group of followers was both astonishing and inspiring. They looked and sounded perfectly fearless in the face of real and enduring danger. They looked and sounded as if they'd found the one thing we all desire: true security.

True security can sometimes resemble the lack of inhibition that comes with drinking alcohol—but only until you look a little closer. The apostles, who had been in hiding for several weeks out of fear for their own lives, had suddenly become completely uninhibited. They literally "put themselves out there" and proclaimed in loud and clear voices their allegiance to Jesus Christ. Such a lack of inhibition is characteristic of those who "reside" in the kingdom of God. In chapter 5, we'll more fully explore what makes this form of inebriation unique, but let's preview it now so that we can begin to recognize it in others.

Because of their true security, kingdom-dwellers are totally uninhibited when it comes to

- putting their own needs aside to tend to the needs of others.
- having a lightness of being; they're not flippant, but they have the ability to brighten up a room.
- living in a state of serenity; even in the midst of turmoil, they're unflappable.

- winking at the foibles and shortcomings of others instead of putting people in their place.
- responding to even the grumpiest of people with graciousness and civility.
- keeping the best interests of others in mind, even when they fail us.
- staying on message even under duress.
- remaining even-keeled and reasonable in the face of conflict.
- practicing mindfulness.

These are the traits and characteristics of kingdom-dwellers—people who have a profound sense of security because they know they live under the protection of an ever-present king who has their best interests in mind. This kingdom takes great imagination to recognize.

Unfortunately, imagination often gets a bad rap and is distrusted as an escape hatch from reality, when in fact it is the capacity to see *beyond* and *through* the reality that meets the eye to a higher one. Indeed, Jesus literally embodied the imaginative reality of the kingdom of God. This is not to say that Jesus' proclamation of the kingdom is a fairy story. What it means is that it takes great imagination to recognize the blessings of being poor, of peacemaking, of being meek, of mourning, of hungering for justice, and of being persecuted for righteousness' sake. It takes great imagination to turn the other cheek, to love your enemies, and to pray for those who persecute you. And yet, despite the challenge, Jesus tells us that such imaginings will lead us to the kingdom of God, that this kingdom is our ultimate destiny, and that its reality is within our grasp. To follow Jesus, then, is to begin a journey that won't require your body to move an inch but that will require your spirit to lean in toward the place where the seeds of the kingdom reside—within your heart.

The kingdom of God is a reality that is in our midst, albeit unseen. And yet, by his very existence—his incarnation—Jesus held this unseen reality before our very eyes. It is to the person of Jesus that we now turn our attention.

2

An Unusual Poster Child

The Face of the Kingdom

I am the way, and the truth, and the life.
—John 14:6

When it comes to your future, financial planners tell you it's wise to invest. There are two problems with this advice. First of all, you need to be lucky enough to have a few spare nickels in hand. And second, it's hard to know whom you can trust with your investment. Any investment involves a risk, and it's hard to put your personal risk in the hands of an impersonal company. We want to see a real face and be persuaded that he or she cares. This is precisely why an investment firm such as Charles Schwab might use the motto "Talk to Chuck"; "Chuck" is how you would address a friend named Charles, and friends can be trusted.

Of course, money is not the only thing that we need to invest as we look to the future. Where and in whom will we invest our energies? Our time? Our compassion? Our dreams? The invitation to the alternate reality that we call the kingdom of God is an invitation to make an investment. But it's an investment that sounds risky at first. Can this kingdom be trusted? Can we see its portfolio? Who is the face of this kingdom? It might be wise to set up an appointment to meet this person in the flesh.

In the Flesh

For my fiftieth birthday, my wife told me to splurge and buy a ticket to see Sir Paul McCartney live at Wrigley Field in Chicago. Even after John Lennon's tragic death in 1980, I still held out hope for an opportunity to see one of the remaining Beatles perform in the flesh. My wish came true, and it was one of the highlights of my life—something to cross off the old bucket list.

We all long to see certain people in the flesh. This desire is never more poignant than when children long to see one of their parents return from military service. Writing letters, texting, e-mailing, and Skyping are all nice, but to see a parent in the flesh and to hold them once again is divine.

Throughout history, humankind has deeply desired to see God's "face." God knew the best way for such an encounter to happen was in the flesh. Jesus Christ is God, in the flesh. He is the face of God. He is to the kingdom what Chuck is to Charles Schwab—someone who can be trusted with your investment. When Jesus spoke about the kingdom of God and people asked him to show them the king, he said, in essence, "Look at me. I am the face of God. I am God in the flesh." To look at Jesus Christ is to gaze directly at the embodiment of the kingdom of God. To use a contemporary analogy, Jesus is the "poster child" for the kingdom of God. But he is an unusual one. He lacks glamour, and he isn't interested in celebrity. He wears no crown but a crown of thorns, and he does not sit not on a throne but hangs from a cross. And yet we proclaim this Jesus as the epitome of life in the alternate reality known as the kingdom of God. This life and this face promise us an incredible return on our investment.

Jesus and the Birthers

Throughout his years of campaigning and then serving in office, President Barack Obama has continually faced charges from a political fringe group that he is not a legitimate citizen of the United States. These "birthers," as they have come to be known, claim that Mr. Obama was born in Kenya, not Hawaii, and they have repeatedly demanded to see his birth certificate. Even though that document has been produced, they continue to clamor for the "long form" of the certificate. Their goal is nothing short of painting President Obama as a fraud.

Jesus faced a similar challenge in his own day. People had firm expectations about what qualities the legitimate and long-awaited "messiah"—the anointed one, the "Christ"—would have. The people of Israel, having watched their once-powerful kingdoms defeated and obliterated, longed for the day when a new king would arrive to lead them back to their home and do all the things a king is expected to do for his people. (See chapter 1.) In fact, in the centuries leading up to Jesus' time, a number of figures were hailed as the messiah, the one who would restore Israel to its rightful place. One by one, however, these would-be messiahs met defeat at the hands of occupying forces and their causes died out. So naturally, when Jesus came along and was rumored to be the messiah, many people responded with skepticism. Was this man Jesus legit, or would he be yet another disappointment in a long line of them?

So what *were* the expectations for a messiah? What were the litmus tests? Scholars N. T. Wright and Robert Barron have identified several specific tasks the Jewish people believed the true messiah would accomplish.

- The messiah would be God's agent, the instrument through which God would fulfill his plan and his promise to return to

Israel, dwell among his chosen people, and bring about salvation for all through them.

- Like any good king, the messiah would gather and unite his people—in this case, the scattered tribes of Israel. He would end their exile, plant them firmly in their home, and remain with them forever. (Although the Babylonian exile ended in 537 BC, the Jewish people had returned to a decimated homeland ruled by an occupying force—not exactly the homecoming they had hoped for. Thus, for all intents and purposes, they were still a people "in exile.")

- The messiah would cleanse the Temple in Jerusalem, which had been abominated by the occupying forces. He would restore it to its rightful place as the symbol of God's presence in the midst of his people and the locus for proper worship of God.

- The messiah would defeat the enemies of Israel—in Jesus' time, the Roman Empire—and in doing so, restore Israel's freedom and autonomy.

These were the expectations that Jesus would be measured against. The "birthers" of his time were skeptical of his legitimacy. "Who is this man?" they asked. "Where does his authority come from? Isn't he the carpenter's son?" In essence, they wanted to see Jesus' "papers" to judge whether he could legitimately be called the messiah. And in retrospect, you really can't blame them. Jesus showed no obvious signs of fulfilling the above expectations, and being executed as a state criminal didn't help. So how is it—why is it—that within days of this convicted criminal's humiliating execution, his followers were to be heard fearlessly and joyfully proclaiming him as the messiah of Israel? So convinced were his followers that Jesus was the real thing, that the authors of the Gospels (Matthew and Luke, in particular) eventually set out to silence the "birthers"—those who remained skeptical—by providing the "long form" of Jesus' "birth certificate": his genealogy. The first followers of Jesus believed without a doubt that Jesus was the anointed one, the "poster child" for the kingdom of God—albeit an unusual one.

The Army You've Got

During the US invasion of Iraq in 2003, reports surfaced that American troops were not being supplied with sufficient armor, and as a result, were vulnerable to roadside bombs. The complaints were leveled not only by civilians but also by military personnel. In response, then-Secretary of Defense Donald Rumsfeld famously retorted, "You go to war with the army you have, not the army you might want or wish to have at a later time." Well, the Jewish people of Jesus' time certainly had their own idea of the messiah they wished to have, and for most, Jesus was not the one they wanted to go to war with (Barabbas, on the other hand, was—but more about that in chapter 4.) In fact, in the days following Jesus' death, even the apostles belonged to this group of skeptics. Their feelings of disappointment were transformed within three days, however; through the lens of the Resurrection, they came to recognize that Jesus had indeed accomplished everything the messiah was expected to accomplish. He just did it in a surprising way.

Early in Luke's Gospel (3:1–2) we are given a clue as to how to approach Jesus with a reversal of expectations. As you read the following passage, imagine it being announced with great fanfare—drum rolls and trumpet blasts—and a loud booming voice like boxing-ring announcer Michael Buffer's *"LLLLLet's get ready to rumble!"*

IN THE FIFTEENTH YEAR OF THE REIGN OF EMPEROR TIBERIUS, WHEN PONTIUS PILATE WAS GOVERNOR OF JUDEA, AND HEROD WAS RULER OF GALILEE, AND HIS BROTHER PHILIP RULER OF THE REGION OF ITURAEA

AND TRACHONITIS, AND LYSANIAS RULER OF ABILENE,
DURING THE HIGH PRIESTHOOD OF ANNAS AND
CAIAPHAS . . .

Now, imagine the music comes to a screeching halt and the loud,
booming voice is silenced, followed by a quiet, almost bewildered voice
that completes the sentence by saying,

the word of God came to John son of Zechariah in the wilderness.

Finally, cue the crickets and tumbleweeds.

If you catch my drift, you know that Luke was announcing that all
bets were off. All expectations were about to be reversed. The "legitimate" leaders and powers-that-be were about to be bypassed by God,
whose mighty word would come instead to a "nobody" in the desert
who, in turn, would announce the coming of the one for whom Israel
had been waiting—the one who would fulfill all of Israel's expectations
in a very unexpected way and without possessing any political power
whatsoever. Jesus' challenge, and the challenge of his early followers,
then, was to demonstrate that his unorthodox approach was indeed
capable of fulfilling the Jews' expectations for the messiah, and in fact,
was the *only* way those expectations could truly be fulfilled.

Let's take a look at how they did this by considering each expectation in turn.

The messiah would be God's agent.

Jesus not only met but exceeded this expectation, presenting himself
not as God's agent but as the very face of God: "Whoever has seen me
has seen the Father" (John 14:9). He proclaimed that it was through
him that God had indeed returned to his people, was fulfilling his
plan, and was living among them: "And the Word became flesh and
lived among us" (John 1:14). As God among them, Jesus would bring

about salvation for all: "I am the way, and the truth, and the life." (John 14:6)

The messiah would gather and unite his people.

In the Old Testament, one of the most profound effects of sin is scattering. The sins of Adam and Eve, Cain and Abel, and the folks who attempted to build the Tower of Babel—to name just a few—resulted in the scattering of people and the breaking of relationships. When Jesus announced that the kingdom of God was near, he was proclaiming the end of the scattering. Jesus embodied this gathering—another reversal—in reaching out to those who had been scattered to the margins of society: lepers, Samaritans, women, tax collectors, the poor, and so on. Jesus gathered and dined with these outcasts so often, in fact, that he was accused of being a drunk and a glutton himself (see Luke 7:34). To eat with the marginalized was to bring them back into the covenant, back into unity with God's people.

The messiah would cleanse the Temple in Jerusalem.

The expectation that the messiah would "cleanse the Temple" was not that he would come along with a Swiffer mop and tidy things up after years of neglect. To "cleanse the Temple" meant to remove the abominations that the occupying forces had brought there—primarily, the worship of other gods—and to restore pure worship to the Temple. When Jesus entered Jerusalem and was welcomed as a king (more about that shortly), he headed straight for the Temple, formed a whip out of cords, and overturned the tables of the money changers, claiming that his Father's "house" had been turned into a "den of robbers" (Matthew 21:13). This act is referred to as the "cleansing of the Temple"; however, it was not directed solely at the money changers, nor was it primarily about dishonest business practices or the impropriety of money changing in the shadows of the Holy of Holies. Jesus' dramatic act was intended to send a stinging message to the people of Israel, the message that *they* were the "den of robbers" sullying the Temple. He was announcing that it was an abomination for them to believe Temple worship (for us, "going to church") was the extent of their duties and granted them license to behave in contradictory ways outside its walls. Jesus wasn't trying to be a one-man Better Business Bureau, sweeping in to expose dishonest practices or irreverent behavior taking place in the Temple foyer. Instead, he was not-so-subtly signaling that this form of worship as a whole was at an end. Without the money changers, the worshippers could not proceed with their sacrifices, and the entire system would come to a standstill. And the only people who had the authority to enforce a new form of Temple worship were the high priest of the Temple and the king of Israel.

Which brings us back to Jesus' entry into Jerusalem. Too often, this triumphant entrance is seen as almost accidental—as if Jesus and his apostles were merely on a pilgrimage to Jerusalem and were suddenly surprised by throngs of adoring fans. Not so. This was a completely choreographed event—a "campaign stop," if you will, along Jesus' route leading to his ultimate destination, Jerusalem. By entering this holy city on a donkey (as prophesied in Zechariah 9:9), Jesus was proclaiming himself the long-awaited king—an act the crowds loved because, by cheering for this king rather than for Caesar, they could stick it to the Romans, whom they disdained. And so, for their own less-than-noble reasons, they greeted Jesus royally: they spread their cloaks on the road, indicating loyalty; they waved palm branches, which was an expression of acclamation; they sang hymns invoking King David. (The word *hosanna,* by the way, is not only an expression of praise but also of urgent need: "Please, save us!") No, Palm Sunday, as we have come to call it, was no accident; it was a triumphant event for Jesus. Likewise, the cleansing of the Temple was no impulsive fit of anger on Jesus' part. It was his signal that one particular messianic function was being fulfilled and that the kingdom of God was in full bloom. It is for this reason that the Letter to the Hebrews refers to Jesus as "a great high priest" (4:14): he was accomplishing what normally would have been the responsibility of the high priest of the Temple—that is, ensuring pure worship.

The messiah would defeat the enemies of Israel.

"How the heck do you rationalize this one?" you may be wondering. The crucified Jesus certainly did not appear victorious in his battle with Israel's enemy, the Roman Empire. If Jesus was truly a king, he seems to have forgotten one small detail: an army! It's no surprise that Pontius Pilate's interrogation of Jesus—"Are you the King of the Jews?" (John 18:33)—implied this unstated question: "So, where's your army?" Jesus, of course, responded that he had an army but one that was not of this world—an answer that didn't sit well with Pilate.

What kind of army was Jesus talking about and what kind of a warrior was he? Again, the Gospel of Luke provides some clues. Luke's infancy narrative makes it clear that Jesus was born to do battle. The story is set in Bethlehem, the hometown of the great warrior king, David, and it begins by identifying the worldly powers, namely, Caesar Augustus and Quirinius, governor of Syria (think Michael Buffer's voice once again). As in Luke's introduction to John the Baptist, however, this preamble (see 2:12) is not really about the powers that be, but instead about another king, one born in a very unusual palace—a stable, with actual crickets and tumbleweeds—and "seated" on a very unusual throne: a manger.

Meanwhile, this new king's unlikely army is assembling. Luke tells us that shepherds in a nearby field are terrified by the appearance of a host of angels. Why be frightened by a bunch of fluffy, white-winged spirits gently hovering and strumming their harps, you ask? Get that image out of your head. What the shepherds saw was an army prepared for battle—an intimidating sight, indeed, more like an army of Orcs from *The Lord of the Rings* than an airborne Vienna Boys' Choir.

The Gospels proceed to tell us how the adult Jesus, during his three years of public ministry, engages the enemies of Israel, who turn out to be not the powers of the Roman Empire but the powers of sin and evil and their ultimate weapon, death. This epic battle culminates in the final confrontation in Jerusalem, where Jesus unveils a new weapon, the cross (more about that in chapter 4), as well as a new strategy: nonviolent, selfless love. Even so, we might wonder where Jesus' army disappeared to when their leader charged headlong into battle. In an easy-to-miss moment of Jesus' passion, Luke reminds us that Jesus' army is, in fact, right where it needs to be. As Jesus struggled with anguish and doubt in the Garden of Gethsemane, "an angel from heaven appeared to him and gave him strength" (Luke 22:43). Jesus' army *was* with him, though it wasn't visible to the mortal eye. In the end, what looked to Jesus' enemies like his defeat was really the first moment of his victory over the greatest enemies of Israel: sin and its offspring, death. This explains why Jesus uttered the words "It is finished" from the cross: he was in essence saying "mission accomplished"—not words of defeat, but of victory.

A Very Tall Order

The Jews expected their messiah to fill a very tall order—and so it comes as no surprise that Jesus' identity is uppermost in the minds of those with whom he comes into contact during his ministry. Consider, for example, the following queries, all recorded in the Gospel of Mark:

- "What is this? A new teaching—with authority! He commands even the unclean spirits, and they obey him" (1:27).
- "Why does this fellow speak in this way? It is blasphemy! Who can forgive sins but God alone?" (2:7).

- "Who then is this, that even the wind and the sea obey him?" (4:41).

- "Where did this man get all this? What is this wisdom that has been given to him? What deeds of power are being done by his hands! Is not this the carpenter, the son of Mary and brother of James and Joses and Judas and Simon, and are not his sisters here with us?" (6:2–3).

- "Are you the Messiah, the Son of the Blessed One?" (14:61).

- "Are you the King of the Jews?" (15:2).

Curiously—or maybe not—the only ones who are absolutely sure of Jesus' identity are his enemies, the evil spirits and demons he casts out from people.

- "What have you to do with us, Son of God? Have you come here to torment us before the time?" (Matthew 8:29).

- Whenever the unclean spirits saw him, they fell down before him and shouted, "You are the Son of God!" (Mark 3:11).

- "What have you to do with me, Jesus, Son of the Most High God?" (Mark 5:7).

- "What have you to do with us, Jesus of Nazareth? Have you come to destroy us? I know who you are, the Holy One of God" (Mark 1:24; Luke 4:34).

- "What have you to do with me, Jesus, Son of the Most High God? I beg you, do not torment me" (Luke 8:28).

- Demons also came out of many, shouting, "You are the Son of God!" But he rebuked them and would not allow them to speak, because they knew that he was the Messiah (Luke 4:41).

Jesus' enemies recognize him as the only one who can defeat them; thus, they dread him. Meanwhile, his friends and followers seem unable to grasp this truth. Perhaps out of curiosity and perhaps out of impatience, Jesus asks his disciples, "Who do people say that I am?" (Mark 8:27). After the disciples hem and haw and mumble something about John the Baptist, Elijah, and the prophets, Jesus grows more direct: "But who do you say that I am?" (8:29).

Jesus poses the same question to us: "Who do you say that I am?"

Our answer betrays whether or not we are ready to invest in him. Like the disciples and his other Jewish followers, we are invited to declare, without hesitation, that Jesus is the Messiah, the face of God, and the fulfillment of our deepest hopes and desires. We are invited to recognize that, as Pope John Paul II taught, "the kingdom of God is not a concept, a doctrine, or a program . . . but it is before all else a person with the face and name of Jesus of Nazareth, the image of the invisible God." There's no getting around it: entrance into the alternate reality that we call the kingdom of God occurs in and through a relationship with Jesus Christ. Friendships do that; they call us into a new reality. And the best vantage point from which to recognize this new reality is the foot of the cross—the same vantage point from which the Roman centurion, having witnessed Jesus' ultimate act of selfless love, exclaimed, "Truly this man was God's Son!" (Mark 15:39). In the end, it is not only Jesus' words but primarily his actions—his mighty deeds—that give us the evidence we need to conclude with confidence that he is God in the flesh, worthy both of the title "Lord" and of being entrusted with the investment of our hearts and lives.

It is to these mighty deeds of the Lord that we now turn.

3

Show Me a Sign

Jesus' Mighty Deeds

The blind receive their sight, the lame walk.
—Matthew 11:5

One of the worst feelings in the world is *powerlessness*. It's the feeling a child has when he or she is being bullied. It's the feeling an adult has when faced with the loss of a job and mounting bills. It's the feeling an elderly person has when they've fallen and can't get up. It's the feeling that people have when they find themselves lying in a hospital bed, unsure of their prospects for recovery. The truth is, all fear is grounded in the perception of powerlessness. When we become empowered or feel empowered, our fears evaporate.

Unfortunately, we humans too often seek empowerment by responding to threats with a bigger, more powerful version of the very threat we fear. In the movie *My Bodyguard*, for example, young Clifford Peache (played by Chris Makepeace) is terrified at the prospect of going to his new school, where he is being extorted by the school bully, Moody (played by Matt Dillon). Clifford "hires" a body-guard, Linderman (Adam Baldwin), a big, tough-looking but sullen kid rumored to have murdered his own brother. With his bodyguard at his side, or at least nearby, Clifford is empowered to go to school without fear—until Moody hires someone even bigger than Linderman to whip Linderman's butt. The cycle simply continues.

On a more tragic note, when twenty-six innocent lives—children and teachers—were killed in the Newtown, Connecticut, massacre in 2012, gun sales soared in the ensuing days, just as they had following similar mass shootings at Columbine, Aurora, Virginia Tech, Northern Illinois University, and Fort Hood. In the wake of the Newtown killings, the National Rifle Association responded to the tragedy in Newtown by calling for school personnel to be armed, claiming, "the only thing that can stop a bad guy with a gun is a good guy with a gun." Burdened by the horrible sense of powerlessness that we feel in the wake of such tragedies, we often—impulsively—seek to respond by arming ourselves with a more powerful version of the very same weapon we claim to loathe. On the surface, this may sound reasonable: bigger guns in the hands of good guys will defeat bad guys with smaller guns. The only problem is that the "solution" is an illusion. Eventually a bigger gun in badder hands will come along and the cycle of violence and fear will be perpetuated.

On a day-to-day basis, the "violence" inflicted upon most people in our country does not involve guns. Instead, we find ourselves being "wounded" by gossip, jealousy, angry words, passive-aggressive behavior, power moves, rudeness, or cold shoulders. In the face of these threats, we often feel powerless. In response, we can do one of three things:

- lapse into cynicism, negativity, or despair over our powerlessness;
- respond with a more aggressive form of the very behavior that was inflicted upon us; or
- ally ourselves with someone who is capable of warding off or defeating those behaviors that threaten us.

At the heart of the Christian gospel is the invitation from Jesus to ally ourselves with a power that is capable of defeating that which threatens us most, evil—not through a bigger, more powerful version of evil, but through an alternative power: the proactive, nonviolent love that prevails in the kingdom of God.

The Big Four

Few things bring us face-to-face with our sense of human powerlessness in a more intense way than the following:

- sickness (in mind, body, or spirit)
- lack of sustenance (job, food, housing)
- natural disasters
- death

And while few of us continue to believe, as folks did in biblical times, that these things occur as punishment for our individual sins, we do have a gnawing sense that they are mysteriously representative of evil in general and of all that is in opposition to God, who alone possesses the power to overcome them and the threats they pose. To demonstrate this reality, Jesus devoted his three years of public ministry to performing dramatic actions—mighty deeds—that revealed his power over these dark realities. His mighty deeds announce to us an alternate reality in which we are no longer powerless: our "bodyguard" has arrived and is in our midst so that we no longer need to fear. That which threatens us in the present cannot and will not stand up to the power of God in the long run. So, just as sickness, lack of sustenance, natural disasters, and death represent that which is in opposition to God, Jesus' mighty deeds—healing the sick, casting out demons, changing water to wine, multiplying loaves and fishes, calming storms, and raising the dead—represent that which overwhelms these threats: the presence of God in our midst. Armed with such power, we become capable of responding to threats with the same confident attitude that St. Paul expressed: "We are afflicted in every way, but not crushed; perplexed, but not driven to despair; persecuted, but not forsaken; struck down, but not destroyed" (2 Corinthians 4:8–9).

Jesus' mighty deeds were not the result of his desire to do nice things for people. Instead, they were strategically performed to announce a new reality, one that he would later entrust his followers with the responsibility of spreading through similar deeds of their own. Before we turn to that responsibility—which is, in fact, ours—let's look more closely at the idea that Jesus' mighty deeds were strategic pointers to the kingdom of God.

Image Is Everything?

Image is everything. On the surface, this may sound shallow and superficial, as if I were claiming that a lack of substance is fine as long as you look good. However, I'm merely stating a fact: we perceive reality by encountering images through our senses, and we formulate judgments accordingly. Unfortunately, this reality is often cynically exploited—by advertisers, politicians, and even some varieties of religion. Jesus, however, understood the power of image and perception and used it to draw attention to the substance of his message. With no help from a marketing specialist, Jesus created precisely the image he intended to create through performing his mighty deeds. Ultimately, Jesus met his death not because his image was misunderstood, but because his image as the face of God was communicated all too well—and therefore perceived both as blasphemy and as a threat to the status quo.

To say that Jesus was the master image-maker, however, is not to say that everything he did was just for show. Of course he was driven by mercy and compassion, but he was no mere humanitarian. Jesus was also keenly aware of how his words and actions would be perceived.

And he wanted to be sure they were perceived as the heralding of a new reality, one whose king and army were equipped with the only weapons capable of truly overthrowing the powers of this world.

Jesus' mighty deeds proved so strategic that the Gospel of John refers to them as *signs*—signs pointing to the in-breaking of the kingdom of God. Signs are not posted by accident. They are posted in order to draw attention and communicate a message. Too often, however, we miss the very signs that are right in front of our nose. In the movie *Bruce Almighty*, for example, the character played by Jim Carrey experiences the worst day of his life. As he drives his car down the street, he desperately begs God to offer him a sign of hope—completely blind to the entire truckload of "Warning" signs right in front of him. We are like this from time to time. The good news is that we can train ourselves to look for the signs that surround us all the time. To begin our training, Jesus not only *talked* about the kingdom of God, he also performed signs that couldn't be missed, signs that revealed the presence of the kingdom in the here and now. While Jesus' mighty deeds were clearly "for show," he did not perform them to impress people or to prove his power, but rather to invite a response.

Nothing up My Sleeve

For as long as there have been human beings with imaginations, magicians have captured the fancy of anyone willing to watch. Magicians are entertainers who create illusions intended to mystify and baffle their audiences. The illusion is that they are performing their actions by means of a connection with the supernatural. The implication is that they are doing something outside of human capability by using powers that we would normally attribute to God.

Jesus was no magician. He did perform numerous acts that mystified and baffled the crowds; but unlike magicians, who closely guard and conceal the secrets of their "power," Jesus sought to *reveal* the source of his power—his Father in heaven. And not only that, Jesus sought to share that power with others. While magicians perform acts in order to attract fans, Jesus performed signs and actions—mighty deeds—to attract apprentices. In short, his goal was to perform mighty deeds, reveal the source of his power, and empower others to perform similar acts.

While Jesus performed a wide variety of mighty deeds, they can best be understood as belonging to two general categories: *creating* and *redeeming*.

In essence, God does only two things, but, he does them really, really well! Creating and redeeming are the primary functions of God in relation to human beings. God gives life, and God restores meaning to life. And since Jesus is the face of God, it makes sense that, like his Father, he would be proficient in these types of activity as well.

During Jesus' time, many people had come to believe that these two actions of God belonged to the distant past and the distant future: When God made the heavens and the earth long, long ago, he created; and when God someday got around to saving the world, he would redeem. Jesus knew that such thinking was folly, and his mighty deeds were designed to expose them as such—to proclaim that God acted ceaselessly in the present, creating and redeeming in the always-unfolding *now*.

Jesus' mighty deeds also reveal that God's creating and redeeming actions diminish and disempower the "Big Four" threats that we mentioned earlier: sickness, loss of sustenance, natural disasters, and death. Let's look at them one by one to see how.

Jesus' Mighty Deeds of Healing

It's true: being sick stinks. Serious illness is one of the most depressing things we can face in life. Not only does it make us feel powerless, living with illness is contrary to both our desires and God's. God does not send us illness. Rather, sickness and disease entered the world as a result of human sin—not your sin or my sin, but the brokenness and imperfection that is the condition of humanity. Illness, therefore, is emblematic of that which is contrary to God.

It's no surprise, then, that the majority of Jesus' mighty deeds involved curing illnesses of the body, mind, and spirit as a way of announcing that the One who has power over these manifestations of evil is actively in our midst. In the Gospels, Jesus cures the following types of physical maladies:

- fever
- paralysis
- blindness
- leprosy
- dropsy
- hemorrhaging
- deafness
- muteness

Each of these healings is a sign that God is on our side in our fight against these intrusions into his creation. Jesus did not wipe out all disease and illness; that remains for the end of time. However, he did make it clear that we are not alone, nor are we powerless, when we face these maladies. God is with us. These healings also speak to us on a symbolic level; we may be experiencing spiritual forms of paralysis, blindness, deafness, and so on. If Jesus can cure these maladies on the physical level, he is certainly capable of curing them on less visible ones.

It's important here to note another type of healing that Jesus performed: exorcisms. On numerous occasions, as noted earlier, Jesus drove demons out of people. Demons are not a thing of the past, nor are they necessarily of the fantastical variety you might encounter in Hollywood films. They are simply forces opposed to God's will. We all have our own personal demons—forces that compel us to do or experience things contrary to God's desires. Fear, for example, is a demon. Anxiety is a demon. Addiction is a demon. The well-known sins of pride, envy, anger, greed, gluttony, lust, and sloth are all demons. And we all suffer the effects of these demons to one extent or another. The exorcisms that are a major part of Jesus' mighty deeds announce with great power that the One who is capable of defeating these enemies of God is in our midst and is actively seeking to share his power over these demons with us.

Jesus' Mighty Deeds of Providing Sustenance

Not knowing when or if the next paycheck will arrive can give rise to acute feelings of powerlessness, especially when you are responsible for the well-being of a spouse and children or other extended family. Even in our affluent society, all too many people find themselves wondering if they will be able to afford food, pay the rent, buy clothing, pay utility bills, or dig out from under a growing mountain of debt. Even those of us lucky enough to have a steady source of income find ourselves wondering if we will be able to pay for our children's college education, handle any future medical bills, and save for retirement. To some extent, we're all susceptible to real or imagined demons of insecurity.

In Jesus' time, the majority of people lived in constant fear of not having enough sustenance for the day ahead. In response to this fear, Jesus' first mighty deed, which took place at the wedding at Cana, was one of providing abundant sustenance. Celebrations are marked by abundance, and so, when the wine supply ran low, the success of the wedding was in jeopardy. Jesus knew that he could use this moment to communicate something important about God—the fact that God provides, and *is,* abundance. It's miracle enough that Jesus changed water into wine, but even more significant is the *amount* of wine he created: six stone jars full, each capable of holding twenty to thirty gallons. That's a lot of wine! Not only did such an abundance of wine make for a good party, it also told the guests, and tells us, that when Jesus is present abundance is guaranteed. And so, although concerns about money and material goods may plague our daily lives, the message is clear. That which we need most—the grace of God—is in no short supply.

The same message is at the heart of Jesus' other mighty deed related to sustenance, namely, the multiplication of the loaves and fishes. The great crowds that followed Jesus brought with them many hungers, not the least of which was physical. They wondered who would ultimately sustain them in their precarious existence. Jesus offered sustenance on many levels that day; however, it was the offering of physical sustenance in the forms of bread and fish that captured the collective imagination of the people there and led them to perceive in Jesus a king who could and would provide for his subjects. What they missed, unfortunately, was the symbolic value of this mighty deed—one that included abundant leftovers. Jesus was not offering "a chicken in every pot"; he was offering *himself.* While all too many people today go to bed physically hungry, many more of us go to bed spiritually hungry, wondering (perhaps unconsciously) what and who will sustain us in the coming day. Jesus' mighty deeds reveal that he alone is to be our source of sustenance—an abundant source that will never be depleted.

Jesus' Mighty Deeds over Nature

Aftermath images of storms such as Katrina and Sandy are heartbreaking. Hurricanes, tornadoes, earthquakes, floods, and other natural disasters all too often leave people in helpless, powerless situations, their homes and communities destroyed. Nature, which God created for the enjoyment of his most beloved creatures, human beings, has also been "infected" by powers that are contrary to God. Natural disasters are reminders of our powerlessness and our need to ally ourselves with a greater power.

Jesus walked upon the water and calmed the storm on the lake in order to reveal that the One who had power over all creation has not abandoned it but is present in and actively maintaining it. Both of these nature miracles communicate the same message: the threats and crises we encounter in nature—all manifestations of the threat of evil—are no match for the power of the Creator, who makes all things new. In essence, they tell us that if God can walk upon the water and calm the wind and waves, he can most certainly help us stay afloat in the turbulent waters of our existence and calm the storms of our lives. It is no coincidence that survivors of natural disasters often attribute the fact of their survival to the grace of God—the only power stronger than the power of nature. While the power of nature is formidable and capable of destroying life, the infinitely greater power of God is capable of creating new life and renewing existing life.

Jesus' Mighty Deeds over Death

If any human experience stands out as totally contrary to God, it is death. God creates and redeems; death was not part of the original plan. Human sinfulness, however, allowed death to enter creation, and it remains the ultimate example of that which is in opposition to God. Fear of death can provoke the most profound feeling of powerlessness possible, as can the death of a loved one. Nothing we do can make us live forever, and nothing we do can bring a loved one back. Because we fear it so deeply and because it *seems* to be the end of existence, humans view death as our ultimate enemy. And like the Washington Generals and the New York Nationals—those hapless exhibition opponents of the Harlem Globetrotters—we seem to be forever stuck on the losing side in the battle against death.

Until Jesus came along, that is. Among his many mighty deeds, the mightiest were his acts of raising people from the dead. Nothing communicates the power and presence of God more than the undoing of death: the death of a widow's son in the town of Nain (see Luke 7), the death of the twelve-year-old daughter of a temple official named Jairus (see Matthew 9), and most famous of all, the death of Jesus' dear friend Lazarus (see John 11). In each case, the message was clear: the only power stronger than death is present among us.

Soon after these amazing events, Jesus' own resurrection provided the most convincing evidence of all that death is not invincible and that he who can overpower it is in our midst. Once and for all, it was made clear to the world that death is not the end—and that we can begin to experience and enjoy *now* the eternal life that we hope to enjoy in its fullness in eternity. Kingdom-dwellers—people who thrive under the influence of the good news of Jesus Christ—live without fear of death because it has been proven illusory by God's mightiest deed: the resurrection of his Son.

It's a Miracle!

You may have noticed that I've used the phrase "mighty deeds" to refer to those amazing actions of Jesus that we typically refer to as *miracles*. This is for good reason. First, the words used in Hebrew and Greek to describe extraordinary occurrences are not easily translated into English. The closest translations are "sign" and "wonder"—which brings me to my second reason for avoiding the word *miracle*. Simply put, our contemporary understanding of a miracle would be anathema to biblical cultures. Today, we consider a miracle to be an *interruption* of the way things normally happen, as if God suddenly decided to get out of his recliner and intervene in a process he typically leaves alone. Since biblical cultures lacked the kind of science we have today, they believed that God was actively and intimately involved in every aspect of his creation: they didn't recognize any distinction between the natural and what we call the supernatural planes. When something extraordinary occurred in nature or in the lives of people, something outside of the expected norm, it was seen not as a sporadic intervention by God but as further proof that God was intimately involved with every detail of his creation. A miracle was not an interruption of normal processes but rather a glaring reminder of God's constant presence and activity in this world. It was not an anomaly but a heightened example of God's ongoing involvement in the lives of his people.

A good comparison can be found in the world of sports. An athlete may go out onto the field, the court, or the ice, day in and day out, scraping, digging, hustling, and doing his or her job without getting much recognition. Occasionally, however, this athlete's efforts may rise to a new level and produce a particularly brilliant, creative, or beautiful play. It's not as if the player had been waiting in the clubhouse or sitting in the stands, more or less ignoring the game, until he or she decided to intervene and perform a dramatic play before receding once again into the shadows. Rather, the dramatic moment is an example of what the coaches and fans knew all along—that this player shows up for work each day, leaves it all on the field, court, or ice, and is capable of making great plays. Likewise, for the people of biblical times, miracles were seen as God having a particularly good day!

None of this is intended to demystify Jesus' mighty deeds or suggest that they were just normal occurrences magnified by admiring eyes. Rather, the perspective I suggest compels us to see Jesus' mighty deeds not as anomalies but as examples of what the power of God's presence offers us on a daily basis. Miracles seem to have occurred more often in biblical times than our own because God's people had eyes that were still capable of recognizing them. In today's world, where many have wrongly concluded that advances in science relegate God further and further into obsolescence, many no longer think of God as being intimately active in the details of everyday life. On the contrary, our ever-deepening knowledge of science should reinforce our intuition that God is present and involved in even the minutest details of reality. It should enable us to see miracles occurring all around us—not as anomalies but as evidence of God's love for all of creation.

It's no accident that one of the gifts of the Holy Spirit is known as wonder, or awe—the ability to see and be amazed by the world as if through the eyes of a child. This kind of experience is illustrated in the final episode of the classic TV comedy *The Office*, when, as the characters leave the building where they have worked together for almost a decade, they each come to recognize how profound their experience has been in what many consider one of the most mundane environments imaginable: the office of a paper company. As she exits the building, the character Pam, played by Jenna Fischer, reflects: "There's a lot of beauty in ordinary things. Isn't that the point?" Indeed, it is.

Vision Therapy Needed to Recognize Jesus' Mighty Deeds

Perhaps your eyesight is not accustomed to recognizing miracles—mighty deeds—in your everyday life. Perhaps the notion of Jesus restoring your sight, healing you from paralysis or uncleanness, calming the storms of your life, or bringing you back from the dead is foreign to you. If so, you may wonder whether some sort of "vision therapy" is possible, some strategy for developing the ability to recognize God's constant activity in your life. The answer is a resounding yes!

One very good way to begin vision therapy is to focus your "eyesight" on the following four areas of life and to ask yourself how God has revealed his presence to you in each of them.

- **Significant people.** Just as God spoke to his people through Moses and the prophets, God often speaks to us through other people. Who are the people in your life who have shaped and influenced you? Who are the people to whom you owe much?

- **Moments of joy (big or small).** Throughout Scripture, people who recognize encounters with God respond to them in terms of great joy. By reversing that process, we can come to recognize encounters with God, too. In other words, by reflecting on moments of joy, whether big or small, we can recognize God's movement in our lives as the cause of those joy-filled moments.

- **Peak moments of grace.** In addition to all the little ways that God has manifested his presence to us, each of us can think of a handful of extraordinary moments in our lives when we felt we had come face-to-face with the infinite—moments when God's presence was almost palpable. Perhaps it was a brush with death, a moment of incredible luck or fortune, a dramatic recovery from an unfortunate situation, or an extraordinary experience of beauty. Moments like these make us aware of a power greater than our own.

- **Milestones in life.** Each of us can name moments in our lives when we reached a major milestone—a graduation, a new job, a promotion, a birthday or anniversary, or a wedding day, for example. These events cause us to pause and express gratitude, and when we express gratitude, we are touching the Holy, the Giver of all good gifts.

Once you have engaged in this type of reflection and reminiscence and identified the myriad ways God has been active in your life, you can go back and identify which of these events have been experiences of the Lord healing you, providing sustenance for you, revealing his great power to you, and restoring you to life. Then you will be able to proclaim to others, as did the author of "Amazing Grace," that "I once was lost, but now am found; was blind, but now I see."

A Word or Two about Jesus' Words

In this chapter, we have focused on Jesus' actions—his mighty deeds—as the element of his ministry that most forcefully captured the attention and imagination of the crowds. And indeed, it was Jesus' mighty deeds that made him renowned throughout Judea and incited great crowds to follow him. It is crucial, however, that we not minimize the importance of Jesus' words. While Jesus was no mere philosopher or teacher, his words were inextricably linked to his mission of announcing the presence of the kingdom of God. And while we do not have space here to do an in-depth study of the words of Jesus, we can describe his central message, whether in the form of teachings, discourses, or parables, with one word: *accessibility*. Jesus' words reveal to us that we have direct access to a God who is neither remote nor distant, but *present*.

Think about it. Jesus taught us to pray to God using the word *Abba,* an expression of intimacy akin to calling God *Papa*. He taught what we call the "Our Father" in order to remind us that we have direct access to God. Jesus told parables that present an image of God as one who is relentlessly searching us out and as one who takes great joy in our return to his arms. Our God is not one who is aloof, withdrawn, or reserved. Rather, he is in pursuit of us and will not be satisfied until he has drawn us closer to him. It is no accident, either, that Jesus shared most of his words in the context of meals, most often with people considered outcasts by the rest of society. Jesus' words, both spoken and implied, announce that we have direct access to God who is in our midst, and that, through contact with this God, we will experience his mighty deeds.

And Now It's Our Turn

In his book *The Power of Habit*, Charles Duhigg tells the story of how Pepsodent toothpaste became a best-selling product in the early 1900s—a time when few people brushed their teeth. Before long, however, people were using the phrase "Pepsodent smile" to refer to a set of pearly whites. The fact is, Pepsodent had no secret ingredients that cleaned teeth better than any other formula on the market. It did, however, contain ingredients that created a tingling sensation in one's mouth and left a minty aftertaste—a tingling and a taste that people began to crave as part of their oral hygiene routine. It seems that people need some kind of a sign that a product they are using is working, and Pepsodent's ingredients provided that sign.

In a similar way, if we want to promote the message of Jesus to others, we need to recognize that people require some kind of evidence—a sign—that Jesus' message is effective. Does this mean that our own proclamation of the gospel must be accompanied by mighty deeds? We don't typically possess the ability to heal blindness, cast out demons, cure lepers, multiply loaves and fishes, walk on water, or raise the dead. And yet, the answer is a definitive YES! The mighty deeds or signs we are called to "perform," however, won't (in most cases) be spectacles but rather reassurances that God is present and accessible in and through this world: no small miracle, but absolutely doable. Indeed, the message of the gospel is that, when it comes to proclaiming the kingdom, what needs to be done *can* be done. The key for followers of Jesus is to reveal evidence of a transformed life—our own. Jesus said that his followers would continue to perform his works and indeed would perform greater works. In essence, he was saying that revealing a transformed heart is, in a way, an even mightier deed than changing water to wine or multiplying loaves and fishes.

The fact is, the small act of kindness, mercy, or compassion that you show may very well be the miracle that someone in despair has been praying for. This reality is portrayed powerfully and poignantly in the classic musical *Les Miserables*. In this story, Jean Valjean is released from jail on parole after twenty years of hard labor. Unable to find work, Valjean resorts to criminal behavior to survive until he is welcomed into the home of a compassionate bishop who feeds him and gives him a warm bed to sleep in. Valjean, unfortunately, repays the bishop's generosity by running off with his precious silver. When the police catch Valjean and drag him back to the bishop to press charges, the bishop tells the police that he has given the silver to Valjean as a gift and that Valjean accidentally left behind two silver candlesticks, as well. Inspired by this undeserved act of kindness, Valjean experiences "vision therapy": he sees for the first time another way of living. As a result, he commits to turning his life around, becoming an honest man, and showing similar compassion to others. When his days on earth are over, Valjean approaches the gates of heaven and is greeted by none other than the kindly bishop himself. "To love another person is to see the face of God," the bishop remarks. In other words, it's the best path to salvation.

And so it falls to us to help others see the face of God through the mighty deeds that we perform, especially in the areas I referred to earlier as the "Big Four"—sickness, lack of sustenance, natural disasters, and death. The church has come to call mighty deeds in response to these hardships the Works of Mercy. On a physical level, such deeds are known as Corporal Works of Mercy: tending to people's hunger, thirst, sickness, material want, homelessness, and imprisonment. On a spiritual and emotional level, they are known as the Spiritual Works of Mercy: tending to people's lack of knowledge, doubt, despair, mourning, harmful behaviors, and ruptured relationships. As I mentioned earlier, the small acts of kindness we offer to those suffering in these areas will often be perceived as mighty deeds. In sending us forth to do such works, Jesus invites us to become the *imago Dei*—the "image of

God"—for those we encounter, mirroring, as it were, the face of God that Jesus revealed to us through his own words and actions.

Perhaps one of the mightiest deeds witnessed in the past century occurred in 1983 when Pope John Paul II met with Mehmet Ali Agca, the man who had tried to assassinate him two years earlier. The encounter did not involve a dramatic physical healing, the act of walking on water, or the multiplication of loaves and fishes. It consisted only of two men sitting on folding chairs in a jail cell. And yet, in this simple act of forgiveness to an imprisoned man—both a Corporal and a Spiritual Work of Mercy—a window was opened and the world could perceive the face of God, the *imago Dei*.

It is no minor miracle in this day and age for people to be able to say, as the early Christian community once proclaimed, "we have seen his glory" (John 1:14). To live and thrive under the influence of Christ is not primarily to prove or to argue faith, but to proclaim it by way of contagious example. To echo the words of Jesus, if we invite others to "come and see" what the kingdom of God is all about, we had better have something to show them. That something is a transformed heart, one that mirrors the very face of God.

4

Wait, What?

The Cross of Jesus

"If any want to become my followers, let them . . . take up their
cross and follow me."
—Matthew 16:24

When someone wrongs you, it's human nature to want his or her head on a platter—at least on our bad days. I'm not saying this is right or good, I'm just saying it's how we sometimes feel. It's also how we sometimes *act*. Here are some examples.

- On a global level, when Japan attacked Pearl Harbor, the United States responded first by rounding up Japanese Americans and placing them in internment camps, and then, several years later, by obliterating Hiroshima and Nagasaki with atomic bombs. And in doing so, our country felt a sense of righteous retribution.

- In the movies, we applaud the "good guy" when he blows away the "bad guy," and the more violent the retribution, the better we feel. Think *Rambo*, *Die Hard*, *Kill Bill*, or one of your personal favorites. One of *my* favorites is the final fight scene in *Star Trek: The Search for Spock*. In that scene, Admiral Kirk repeatedly and viciously kicks his hateful Klingon adversary in the face, shouting, "I [kick] have had [kick] enough of YOU [kick]!"—finally sending the loathsome creature over a cliff to his well-deserved demise. In Kirk's defense, it must be said that the Klingon had killed Kirk's son—which also explains (if not excuses) how good the scene makes me feel.

- On an even more personal level, back in the eighth grade, when Peter Ochoa scored the winning goal to defeat my team in the school floor-hockey play-offs, I responded by following him into the locker room and kicking his ass. Literally. I buried my foot in his derriere. Man, did that feel good.

Bottom line: it's human nature to want revenge, and when we choose to act, we usually employ a bigger and more powerful version of the same "weapon" that was used against us. It never works—which is a big clue to the fact that human nature is flawed.

The Barabbas Cycle

To the Jews of Jesus' day, the Romans were the Japanese, the Klingons, and Peter Ochoa all wrapped into one. The Jewish people had been living under Roman oppression for far too long and wanted nothing more than Caesar's head on a platter. So, when Pontius Pilate brought forth two prisoners—Jesus and Barabbas—and asked the crowds which one they wanted as their savior, they shouted, "Give us Barabbas!" Why? Because Barabbas was a real-life action hero of the day. In the eyes of the Romans, he was a murderer and an insurrectionist; but in the eyes of the Jews, he was the good guy. He was their Admiral Kirk—the guy who, if ever given the chance, would kick Caesar repeatedly and viciously in the face.

Jesus, on the other hand, appeared to the crowds as the equivalent of the "anti-Rambo"—someone with no army, weapons, or plan of action. Interestingly enough, the name *Barabbas* means "son of the father." Jesus, of course, had referred to himself as the Son of the Father. So when Pilate presented Jesus and Barabbas to the crowds, he was in one sense asking them which "son of the father"—which kind of a messiah or savior—they wanted: an "action hero" who had access to weapons that could bring down the bad guy, or an "antihero" who appeared completely unarmed? The crowds, not surprisingly, chose Barabbas.

Of course, Pilate's question is directed at us, too. Which kind of hero do we want? As Christians, we formally worship Jesus on Sunday; but all too many of us continue to clamor for Barabbas the other six days of the week. We do so because we trust that his weapons are more suited to "the real world" than are those of Jesus Christ. As a result, we remain enslaved by what I call the "Barabbas cycle." Whenever we perceive that we are "attacked" by an evil, we are inclined to respond with a bigger, stronger (but in our eyes more righteous) version of the same evil. Ironically, our actions are self-defeating. By perpetuating evil, we are only strengthening the enemy we aim to crush.

The Gospels, of course, tell us that choosing Barabbas is a mistake—that Jesus is the Savior we need, and that his weapon, the cross, is more powerful than any gun.

The cross? Cue those crickets again.

Unfortunately, many of us Christians tend to tune out the fact that the cross is a weapon, a strategy for confronting evil. As a result, it becomes little more than a sentimental symbol—a decoration, a brand, a shiny thing to wear on a necklace. Or it becomes a mildly pesky reminder of the fact that Jesus died a horrible death, he did it for me, and as a result I owe him one. What's missing in both cases is an understanding that the cross is the most potent weapon known to humanity—and that, just like the kingdom of God, it is constantly at our disposal.

Why do we miss this fact? Because we secretly think of the cross as a symbol of weakness and defeat. To recognize it as a symbol and agent of power is entirely counterintuitive.

A Counterintuitive Strategy

You find yourself stuck in a traffic jam on a crowded expressway on a hot summer day. Even with the AC on full blast, you're sweating. You've got the stereo cranked up to distract you from gridlock boredom. As luck would have it, you glance at the temperature gauge and see that your engine is overheating. Your first impulse is to power everything down to decrease the strain on the engine and allow it to cool. And yet, strangely enough, the most effective strategy is to do the opposite: to open your windows and turn your heat and blower up to high! Doing so draws heat away from the engine and funnels it into the passenger area where, with the windows open, it can escape, thus cooling down the engine. Because it goes against your every impulse, this strategy can be described as counterintuitive.

Other examples of counterintuitive strategies include

- setting controlled fires to curtail an out-of-control wildfire.
- teaching first-responders to run toward gunfire.
- sailing toward the open sea instead of the harbor to avoid a sudden storm.
- flying a plane higher rather than lower as conditions deteriorate.
- swimming parallel to the shore instead of toward it to escape an undertow.
- allowing children to learn from mistakes rather than keeping mistakes from happening.
- turning the steering wheel to the left instead of the right if the back end of the vehicle skids left on snow or ice.
- speaking quietly to get attention in a noisy room.

Or how about this one? *Dying in order to gain new life.*

This may be the most counterintuitive strategy of all—which is why Christianity is so challenging and often misunderstood, even by those who call themselves Christians. At the heart of Christianity is the paradox of the cross, and there's no getting around it. In order to live, we must die. Jesus said that anyone who wishes to be his disciple must pick up his or her cross every day and follow him.

In fact, the Gospels teach us that, if we want to recognize what God "looks like," we should look to the cross, because this is where God reveals himself most fully: in selfless love. Mark's Gospel, in particular, steers us in this direction. As discussed in chapter 2, Jesus' identity is continually questioned in Mark's Gospel by those who encounter him—and it is precisely at the foot of the cross that these inquiries are answered. Upon witnessing how Jesus died, an unnamed Roman centurion asserts: "Truly this man was God's Son!" (Mark 15:39). Jesus' true identity as the face of God is revealed most clearly at the moment he gives up his life on the cross.

Why then? Why there? Because the event of the cross embodies the counterintuitive nature of Jesus' teaching as a whole. It sums up the idea that we should "turn the other cheek," love our enemies, pray for our persecutors, wash the feet of others, and die to gain new life—none of which come naturally to humans. The cross is not a "stand-alone" event, separate from Jesus' years of teaching and ministry. Nor is it merely the necessary precursor to Easter morning. The cross was not an unfortunate interruption of Jesus' ministry or mission but is the very culmination of his mission—the drawing together of everything that came before and the only possible gateway to everything that would happen after.

Mission Accomplished?

Soon after the toppling of Saddam Hussein's regime in Iraq in 2003, President George W. Bush famously appeared on an aircraft carrier in front of a huge banner announcing "Mission Accomplished." As it turns out, this conclusion was grossly inaccurate: the conflict in Iraq continued and festered for nearly a decade and ended not with a victory but with a withdrawal of forces. The mission was far from accomplished.

Now imagine this very different scenario. After suffering agony on the cross for six hours, Jesus uttered his final words, "It is finished," and then he died. To the human mind, these words smack of defeat, surrender, and relief, as in "Thank God it's over!" But Jesus wasn't admitting defeat or expressing relief at all. Instead, he was claiming victory. He was saying, "Mission accomplished."

Wait. What? Maybe he was confused. Maybe you think *I* am confused. How could Jesus claim victory while breathing his last, tortuous breath?

In John's Gospel, the Greek word later translated as *finished* is *tetelestai* (see 19:30), which means not "over and done with" but "accomplished," "fulfilled," or "brought to completion." It signifies that a goal has been achieved, that a mission has been accomplished. In fact, it was the word typically stamped on an invoice to signify that a transaction was completed and the debt had been paid.

What exactly did Jesus accomplish by dying on the cross? What transaction did he complete? He paid our "debt." It's a simple concept, although one that's often miscast in terms of an angry father demanding appeasement through the blood of his son. When we look at the bare facts, however, an elegant sequence unfolds:

- Sin (and its ultimate consequence, death) entered the world as a result of human rejection of God's love.

- Sin separates us from God.
- In order for our relationship with God to be repaired, a debt had to be paid. The paying of this debt is known as atonement.
- Historically, atonement was sought through the symbolic offering of animal sacrifices.
- Animal sacrifices were clearly insufficient to convey the depth of our contrition; something more was needed.
- Jesus, as one of us, offered himself in our place, and balance was restored.

In other words, Jesus' death accomplished what we ourselves couldn't manage to do: repair our relationship with God. Through his sacrifice, the debt was paid and the relationship healed. Mission accomplished, once and for all. That doesn't mean that all we have to do now is sit back and relax. It does mean, however, that in our battles with sin, we are now equipped with the most effective weapon known to humankind: divine selfless love. And it is because Jesus accomplished this mission that we are able to live with a new identity: we no longer live as a defeated people (as slaves to sin) struggling to regain our identity. As a result of Jesus' saving act of love, we can live as a victorious people: not because of anything we've done but because of Jesus. We no longer relate to God through the law, with an emphasis on what *we* must do; we now relate to God as friend because of what Jesus did. Our responsibility as Christians—those who are like Christ—is to share the good news of this victory with others. And who doesn't like to identify with a winner?

To identify with Christ is to identify with the one who has accomplished the most important mission of all, in admittedly counterintuitive ways. We no longer have a need for Barabbas and all that he represents, namely, the vain and endless quest to save ourselves by using the very weapons of evil we claim to abhor. Instead, we now wield the only weapon that works: the cross. Because of this cross, we Christians behave a certain way—not to earn or achieve our own salvation, but as a consequence of the salvation that has been won for us. To behave like Jesus, to identify with him, requires that we dis-identify with those ways of living that are contrary to him and his message. It requires that we pick up our cross each day and allow God's grace to deal a deadly blow to any inclinations we still possess that are contrary to the values of the kingdom.

"Pick Up Your Cross Daily"

To many of us, this phrase sounds perfectly pious: We must do as Jesus did. To Jesus' followers, who had yet to see him die on the cross, it must have sounded insane. In contemporary terms, it might have sounded like this: "if anyone wishes to follow me, he must pick up a syringe filled with a lethal injection." In essence, Jesus is telling us that each day we must embrace the very instrument that leads to our death so that we might be reborn. Rather than run away from whatever is "killing us"—whatever is wearing us down, making us angry, or making us sick in mind, body, or spirit—we must turn and face it so that both it and our old self may be defeated—not with bigger, badder weapons, but with acceptance and love. This is why, in Twelve-Step programs, hitting rock bottom is an occasion for hope: only when one comes face to face with defeat is recovery truly possible.

Likewise, to "pick up your cross" is *not* to be confused with patiently bearing up under a burden that life has dealt you: sickness, the loss of a job, the death of a loved one, and so on. While we can and should unite our sufferings to the suffering of Jesus, he doesn't want us to passively endure. Instead, he wants us to open ourselves to the transformation that suffering can bring, knowing that "death" to an old way of life or to an old attachment is necessary if we are truly to be born again. To bear your cross is to embrace any instrument that will crucify your human tendency to respond with anything less than total, selfless love. Indeed, the "way of the cross" is not simply a devotional prayer practiced by many Christians, especially Catholics. It is a way of life—a way of entering the kingdom of God.

Breaking the Barabbas Cycle

A good example of what it means to take up one's cross each day is found in the story of Hall of Fame baseball star Jackie Robinson as portrayed in the movie *42*. When Branch Rickey, the owner of the Brooklyn Dodgers, invites Jackie Robinson to become the first African American to play major league ball, he warns Jackie of the brutality he is about to endure. After describing some possible threatening scenarios, Rickey asks Robinson if he can endure such cruelty without responding. Jackie, who has spent a lifetime standing up for himself, says, "You want a man who doesn't have the guts to fight back?" To which Rickey replies, "I want a man who has the guts NOT to fight back!" The movie goes on to show what Jackie did, in fact, endure, and how he struggled not to respond to the horrific taunts and threats that came his way.

Every time Jackie Robinson bit his tongue, he was picking up his cross: he was embracing the instrument that would execute his tendency to fight back like Barabbas. Such an effort takes superhuman—one might say Christlike—strength. But it's worth it. It enables us to defeat evil with a new weapon, the weapon of total self-giving. To be a follower of Jesus is not to turn a blind eye to evil or to look at the world through rose-colored glasses. Rather, it is to recognize evil, take it seriously, and defeat it through self-giving love. For Jackie and for all of baseball, it was a new beginning, but it couldn't have happened without the old Jackie reaching the "end" of his existence.

Breaking the Barabbas cycle is not easy: old habits die hard. And contrary to the popular notion that habits can be changed in twenty-one to twenty-eight days, experts tell us that it can take up to a year to change old habits and develop new ones. In his book *The Power of Habit: Why We Do What We Do in Life and Business*, Charles Duhigg helps us understand why. He describes what he calls "the habit loop," which goes something like this. When we perform an action for the first time, the brain works very hard to collect all the pertinent information involved, from start to finish, and to store the information in the part of the brain called the basal ganglia. If we continue to do the same action every day, the basal ganglia fills in the details so the rest of the brain can turn its attention to other things. Eventually, the action can be performed "without thinking." In short, our brains are looking for ways to save effort, and forming habits is the key to achieving this.

Thus, Duhigg tells us, whenever we enter a situation, the brain begins looking for "cues" that might suggest which habit to draw from. And so begins "the habit loop" in which we encounter a cue or trigger that leads to a routine and finally a reward. For example: you encounter a fast-food restaurant on your way home (a cue) so you pick up some fast food (a routine) and satisfy your hunger quickly and inexpensively (the reward).

When the cue and the reward get to know one another very well, they give birth to a habit. What's key to remember is that when something becomes a habit, the rest of the brain takes a siesta from thinking about it. As a result, habits—whether physical actions, thoughts, or emotions—are very hard to break.

In order for an old habit to be replaced by a new habit, we need to battle until the old habit is laid to rest. Okay, but fight *how*? According to Duhigg, a habit can be changed when we clearly identify the cues and rewards that encourage it, and then find and cultivate a new habit—a routine or behavior—to replace the old one *while leaving the cues and rewards in place*. In this way, the brain is minimally inconvenienced and therefore willing to accept the replacement.

Let's now consider all this in terms of the habit I call the Barabbas cycle. To break that cycle, if you recall, we need to stop fighting evil with evil; we need to slay our sinful habits so that new ones can replace them. The first step in this process is identifying cues and rewards. Fortunately for us Catholics, the practice known as an "examination of conscience" accomplishes this task beautifully. Like the self-inventory in a Twelve-Step program, an examination of conscience compels you to identify all the reasons you practice a bad habit. The second step is finding a new habit to replace the old one. A crucial ingredient in the sacrament of reconciliation is the assignment of a new habit. The practice of this new habit is called penance. We are called to practice penance in our daily lives, too, by forming new behaviors to replace and repair the damage done by sinful ones. The penance that we are assigned in the sacrament of reconciliation is one new behavior or habit that could be inserted to replace the old habit; something that psychologists call a "competing response."

The third step, cultivating the new habit, is the most important one of all. This process begins, Duhigg says, by creating a new craving that drives a new habit loop. According to Catholic thinking, we are born with a craving for God that is often mistaken as a craving for lesser things. "The desire for God," says the *Catechism*, "is written in the human heart."At our deepest core, we crave to be secure in God's loving and protective embrace. As it turns out, bringing this craving to the forefront of our minds is the key to creating new habits.

Which is to say, it is the key to the kingdom. John the Baptist—who prepared the way for the King himself—made it clear that if a craving for the kingdom is genuine, the cultivation of new habits would follow. When people asked him what they must do to enter the kingdom, he replied by telling them to let old habits die and to put new ones in their place:

"Whoever has two coats must share with anyone who has none; and whoever has food must do likewise." Even tax collectors came to be baptized, and they asked him, "Teacher, what should we do?" He said to them, "Collect no more than the amount prescribed for you." Soldiers also asked him, "And we, what should we do?" He said to them, "Do not extort money from anyone by threats or false accusation, and be satisfied with your wages."

—Luke 3:11–14

Jesus responded similarly when a rich young man expressed a craving for the kingdom: "Go, sell what you own, and give the money to the poor, and you will have treasure in heaven; then come, follow me" (Mark 10:21). Knowing that the habits of acquiring and holding material possessions would be hard to break, the young man went away sad; he had yet to entirely give himself over to his craving for God.

Jesus, however, refused to water down his message just to make it easier on us. In what we can think of as his "keynote address," the Sermon on the Mount (Matthew 5–7), Jesus reiterates at great length the idea that old habits must die and be replaced with habits of the kingdom.

Old Habits (Habits of the World)	New Habits (Habits of the Kingdom)
"You have heard that it was said . . . 'You shall not murder'; and 'whoever murders shall be liable to judgment'" (5:21).	"But I say to you that if you are angry with a brother or sister, you will be liable to judgment . . ." (5:22).
"You have heard that it was said, 'You shall not commit adultery'" (5:27).	"But I say to you that everyone who looks at a woman with lust has already committed adultery with her in his heart" (5:28).

Old Habits (Habits of the World)	New Habits (Habits of the Kingdom)
"It was also said, 'Whoever divorces his wife, let him give her a certificate of divorce'" (5:31).	"But I say to you that anyone who divorces his wife, except on the ground of unchastity, causes her to commit adultery; and whoever marries a divorced woman commits adultery" (5:32).
"Again, you have heard that it was said . . . 'You shall not swear falsely, but carry out the vows you have made to the Lord'" (5:33).	"But I say to you, Do not swear at all, either by heaven, for it is the throne of God, or by the earth, for it is his footstool, or by Jerusalem, for it is the city of the great King" (5:34–35).
"You have heard that it was said, 'An eye for an eye and a tooth for a tooth'" (5:38).	"But I say to you, Do not resist an evildoer. But if anyone strikes you on the right cheek, turn the other also; and if anyone wants to sue you and take your coat, give your cloak as well; and if anyone forces you to go one mile, go also the second mile. Give to everyone who begs from you, and do not refuse anyone who wants to borrow from you" (5:39–42).
"You have heard that it was said, 'You shall love your neighbor and hate your enemy'" (5:43).	"But I say to you, Love your enemies and pray for those who persecute you, so that you may be children of your Father in heaven" (5:44–45).
"Whenever you give alms, do not sound a trumpet before you, as the hypocrites do in the synagogues and in the streets, so that they may be praised by others" (6:2).	"But when you give alms, do not let your left hand know what your right hand is doing, so that your alms may be done in secret . . . " (6:3–4).
"And whenever you pray, do not be like the hypocrites; for they love to stand and pray in the synagogues and at the street corners, so that they may be seen by others" (6:5).	"But whenever you pray, go into your room and shut the door and pray to your Father who is in secret; and your Father who sees in secret will reward you" (6:6).

Old Habits (Habits of the World)	New Habits (Habits of the Kingdom)
"And whenever you fast, do not look dismal, like the hypocrites, for they disfigure their faces so as to show others that they are fasting" (6:16).	"But when you fast, put oil on your head and wash your face, so that your fasting may be seen not by others but by your Father who is in secret; and your Father who sees in secret will reward you" (6:17–18).

Jesus sums up his discourse by saying, "Be perfect, therefore, as your heavenly Father is perfect" (Matthew 5:48). The Greek word used here for *perfect* is more correctly translated as *complete,* as in "having reached its end." Or as in "mission accomplished." The message is clear: to participate fully in the accomplishment of the cross, we must dis-identify with a former, defeated way of living and identify with a new way—a kingdom way—of life. The way to do this is to give in to our craving for God.

Keystone Habits: Three Ways to Pick Up Your Cross

Let's return for a moment to Charles Duhigg and *The Power of Habit.* He specifically describes habits he refers to as "keystone habits," explaining that "success doesn't depend on getting every single thing right, but instead relies on identifying a few key priorities and fashioning them into powerful levers." These "levers" are the keystone habits—those that, when changed, "dislodge and remake other patterns." For example, when people add exercise to their daily schedule, it triggers a domino effect of change in their lives: better sleep, better diet, more energy, and so on. In effect, one good habit makes other good habits follow naturally and even contagiously.

So, which "kingdom habits" should we consider "keystone habits"—those we can and should change as we die to the old life and rise into the new? Here are three suggestions.

1. **Stop the flow of words.** We assert ourselves and our egos by talking. In fact, the ego by definition is that internal voice that yammers incessantly about *me, me, me*. One of the best ways to "pick up our cross daily"—to extinguish our old self, our ego self—is to take some time away from words. When our words cease, the ego is neutralized; it stops shouting, "Give us Barabbas!" At the same time, a space opens up into which God can speak instead. What does he say? He says exactly what we need to hear: that we cannot (and do not have to) save ourselves. He reminds us that this mission has been accomplished for us by Jesus' death on the cross, and that, although we are not worthy of this gift by nature, we have been made worthy of it through grace. This is why Jesus said, "When you are praying, do not heap up empty phrases as the Gentiles do; for they think that they will be heard because of their many words" (Matthew 6:7). It's also why God said through the psalmist, "Be still, and know that I am God!" (Psalm 46:10). Both are God's polite way of saying, "Please shut up, just for a moment." The essence of prayer is silence—which douses the ego as surely as water does fire. It also creates a space into which a host of other good and selfless habits can flow.

2. **Stop the flow of consumption.** When babies are hungry, they cry. That's how we are born: obsessed with our own needs. A consumer society perpetuates this infantile state. It wants to make sure that our focus remains on ourselves and that our wants are perceived as our needs. When we intentionally put the brakes on consuming—whether it be food, drink, sex, or material goods—we are introducing a new habit that challenges the old: we are shifting the focus away from ourselves and our own "needs" and enabling ourselves to be more attuned to the needs of others. In other words, we are shifting from selfishness

to selflessness. And if the cross of Jesus stands for anything at all, it stands for the death of the self and the birth of a new life in God.

3. **Increase the flow of generosity.** One of the most dramatic conversion moments in life is becoming a parent. You no longer get to sleep when you want, eat when you want, or watch TV when you want. You no longer get to come and go as you please. Your money is no longer just for you. And somebody is constantly demanding your attention. You have no choice but to forget yourself. You are compelled to embrace a burden of responsibility—but it's a burden you can't imagine being without. To pick up the cross daily is a similar task. It requires you to grow selfless and to carry a burden of responsibility—but a burden that Jesus says is "light" (Matthew 11:30). Why is it so light? Because we are giving the "heaviness" of ourselves and our own concerns away. One good way to do this (short of parenthood) is through generosity toward others. Generosity enables us to rise above ourselves and to live, as St. Ignatius of Loyola said, as a person for others. Remember, when Jesus proclaimed that the kingdom of God was in our midst, he wasn't saying it was tucked away inside of us; he was saying it was within reach. To grasp something within reach, we must reach out; we must also reach out in order to give. By extending ourselves, we lose ourselves and gain a new life simultaneously. Isn't that cool?

Do any of these strategies—or maybe all three of them together—ring a bell? Traditionally, they are referred to as prayer, fasting, and almsgiving—words that have unfortunately lost their power and become "churchy" over time. To prevent the usual yawns, therefore, I've suggested alternate names for them: stopping the flow of words (prayer), stopping the flow of consumption (fasting), and increasing the flow of generosity (almsgiving). Whatever you call them, though, they are both "kingdom habits" and "keystone habits": they dislodge the old and usher in the new. In other words, they break the Barabbas cycle.

The Ability to Adjust

Hall of Fame pitcher and TV baseball analyst Steve Stone has been around the game of baseball for decades and has seen numerous players come and go. When asked what enables some players to become stars while others with equal talent languish and are soon forgotten, Steve quickly responds that it all comes down to one thing: the ability to adjust. He explains that, when a young hitter enters the league and shows that he can turn on an inside fast ball and hit it a mile, pitchers will eventually begin to throw him a steady diet of outside breaking balls. Superstars, Stone says, are those batters who make the adjustment and learn how to go with the outside breaking ball, taking it to the opposite field. It's all in the ability to adjust.

After Michael Jordan achieved three NBA championships with the Chicago Bulls in the 1990s, he stepped away from the game, announcing his retirement. A year and a half later, however, he shocked the sports world and made a comeback. It was obvious to him and to others, however, that he had lost a step and could not be counted on to drive to the hoop on every play and make a thunderous slam dunk as he used to. Could it be that his days as a star were over? To the surprise of everyone, however, Jordan developed a deadly fade-away jump shot that devastated his opponents. He went on to lead the Bulls to three additional championships with a completely different style of playing than his previous one. The old Michael Jordan was gone, but a new Michael Jordan had been born. It's all in the ability to adjust.

The same is true for us each and every day of our lives. We are called to adjust our lives, putting to rest our selfish tendencies in order that a new "selfless self" might be born. Dr. Martin Luther King Jr. put a unique twist on this notion of "adjustability" when he taught that each of us, as followers of Christ, needs to become "maladjusted" to the sinfulness of the world. In his speech to the annual convention of the NAACP in San Francisco on June 27, 1956, Dr. King called on all people to be maladjusted to a way of life that included lynch mobs, segregation, discrimination, inequalities, excessive militarism, and physical violence. He called people to be maladjusted as was the prophet Amos, who, in the face of injustice, forcefully called for justice to "roll down like waters, and righteousness like an ever-flowing stream" (5:24).

Dr. King was reminding us that the world encourages habits that we all too often adopt uncritically. Instead of considering them in light of the gospel, we simply adjust or conform to them. His call to be "maladjusted" to the evils of the world goes hand in hand with Jesus' call to adjust to the values of the kingdom. Rosa Parks, whose actions sparked the Civil Rights movement in the 1950s, heeded both calls. She refused to abide by the habits of a segregated society when she refused to give up her seat on a bus to a white person. She became maladjusted to society's evils, and as a result, society was transformed. We are called each and every day to pick up our cross—the instrument of our death—as Rosa Parks did. We are called to see to it that habits of selfishness, both ours and society's, are extinguished and replaced with selfless ways.

How the Cross "Works"

Today, there is a lot of discussion about vaccinations and which ones people should or should not have. Vaccinations, of course, are counterintuitive: we inject a healthy person with a vaccine that contains elements of the very disease we are trying to prevent. They work, though, because most vaccines contain a small amount of the disease germ in a weakened or dead state. When this small amount of the germ enters the body, it stimulates the body to create a defense. The antibodies created by the vaccine remember how to fight off the germ, should the real germ enter the body. The result is immunity.

God used similarly counterintuitive logic with the Israelites as they wandered through the desert, dropping like flies from snakebites. When Moses asked God for help, God told him to make a bronze image of a snake and lift it up on a pole so that those who had been bitten would look upon it and recover (see Numbers 21:4–9). In other words, they were told to come eyeball-to-eyeball with the very thing that threatened them, and in doing so, be healed. In a sense, the Israelites were "vaccinated" by the bronze image of the serpent that was lifted up before their eyes.

In the same way, Jesus was lifted up on the cross so that we might gaze upon that which threatens us—death and defeat—and in doing so be healed. The cross of Jesus vaccinates us against the deadly virus of sin, of which death is the ultimate consequence. In order to defeat the twin viruses of sin and death, Jesus had to take them upon himself. The cross stands as a symbol of that which is powerful enough to defeat sin and death: selfless love. It's no wonder we Christians rely on the cross to lead us wherever we go: it has defeated that which we are powerless against.

The Cross Always Leads

When the white smoke billowed out of the Vatican chimney on March 13, 2013, the world knew that a new pope had been elected. Who was he? What did he look like? What would he be like? After the declaration of those joyful words—*Habemus Papam!* ("We have a pope!")—it was announced that Cardinal Jorge Mario Bergoglio of Argentina was our new Holy Father and that he would take Francis as his papal name. But few had any additional knowledge of this man.

He had not been among the *papabili*, the "favorites" for election, nor had he been highly visible in popular church media. Many of us sat glued to our TVs, waiting for the balcony curtains to part and for this new mystery pope to emerge.

When the moment arrived and the curtains opened, the first thing that jumped into my mind was, "That's strange; he looks like a cross." In fact, I *was* viewing a cross. Pope Francis—like all newly elected popes—was led onto the balcony by a raised cross, and only after the cross bearer stood aside did we catch our first glimpse of our new Holy Father.

For Catholics, the moment was not at all unusual: We are always led by the cross. It leads us into church at the opening of Mass and it leads us back out into the world at the end of Mass. This ritual isn't accidental; it's rooted in history. Armies have always marched into battle carrying a symbol—a "standard"—that is designed to do three things: announce the identity of the arriving army, instill confidence in the army fighting under that standard, and strike fear in the hearts of its enemies. (Think of the Roman Eagle or the Nazi swastika.) In the same way, the cross of Jesus announces the arrival of a different kind of army, instills the members of this army—us—with confidence, and provokes fear in the forces of evil that are its enemies.

Strictly speaking, this is ironic. In "real world" terms, a cross would seem to represent weakness, defeat, and humiliation. But for those who have encountered the risen Christ, it does the opposite. It serves as a symbol of victory and of the emergence of a new weapon: selfless love. While the cynics of the world continue to search for ever-bigger guns, those who follow the cross look to end the cycle of violence. Instead of responding with despair to the apparent triumphs of evil, the followers of the cross respond with confident hope that goodness has prevailed, does prevail, and will always prevail. In the words of Dr. King: "Returning hate for hate multiplies hate, adding deeper darkness to a night already devoid of stars. Darkness cannot drive out darkness; only light can do that. Hate cannot drive out hate; only love can do that."

Why Do You People Do That to Yourselves?

A friend of mine used to participate in an interreligious group whose Christian, Jewish, Muslim, and Buddhist members gathered regularly at one another's homes for dialogue. Once, when my friend, a Christian, was hosting, he noticed that the Buddhist was distracted by something. When he asked him about it, the Buddhist pointed to the crucifix on the wall and asked, "Why do you people do that to yourselves?" When asked to clarify, the man continued: "Why do you remind yourselves of suffering? In Buddhism, we seek the cessation of suffering. You seem to relish it!"

Of course, we Christians do not relish suffering; but neither do we necessarily seek its cessation. Instead, we seek its transformation. Christianity does not blithely whistle past the graveyard, but rather passes through it with reverence, recognizing its reality but fixing our eyes on the gate beyond it that leads to new life. The cross and the Resurrection depend on each other: without the Resurrection, the cross is a symbol of defeat; but without the cross, the Resurrection could not have happened. For Christians, the path to fullness of life leads through, not around, suffering and death. It is for this reason that we seek to encounter and minister to those who are suffering and in need: not solely to ease or eliminate their suffering, but to encounter God. While we seek to reveal God's compassion and mercy to them, they reveal to us the face of God in our midst.

While God's true identity is revealed in and through the cross, the story does not end there. We now turn our attention to the resurrection of Jesus—what the cross leads us to.

5

It Can't End Like This!

The Resurrection of Jesus

So whoever is in Christ is a new creation.
—2 Corinthians 5:17, NAB

In the classic sci-fi movie *Close Encounters of the Third Kind*, Roy Neary (played by Richard Dreyfuss), sees a UFO but his wife does not believe him. Soon thereafter, however, Roy grows obsessed with mental images of a mountain, and, in an iconic scene, carves a model of the mountain out of a plateful of mashed potatoes as his wife and children look on in confusion. Roy admits to his family that he is behaving strangely but insists, as he points at the mashed-potato mountain, "This is important. This means something." It turns out later that the mountain is where the first encounter with alien life will take place. (The one it represents, not the mashed-potato one.) At some subconscious level, Roy knew his destiny was leading him to that place.

Roy found himself behaving in a certain way, and he had some foggy notion that what he was doing was related to his future. Which is to say that his (blurry) vision for the future dictated his behavior in the present. The same is true of us Christians. The resurrection of Jesus points us toward a future full of hope: a future in which we, like the risen Christ, will live once again, but with renewed bodies and in a renewed creation. Contrary to popular notions, we are not destined to float on clouds playing harps for all eternity. How boring that would be! In fact, the Christian concept of the future is not primarily about "getting to heaven" to be with Jesus, but about Jesus returning to be with us in our renewed bodies on a renewed earth.

Think about it: the Scriptures are filled with images of heaven breaking into the earthly reality, but not of earthlings escaping to heaven. From burning bushes and parting seas to descending doves and tongues of flame, the flow of action is *from* heaven *to* earth. Our ultimate destiny may indeed be "in" heaven, but Scripture tells us that this heaven will somehow be joined with earth to form a new creation. This is precisely why, when Jesus "ascended" into heaven, an angel appeared to the disciples and said, "Why are you standing there looking at the sky?" (see Acts 1:11). The angel is nudging them to see that their ultimate destiny is not somewhere in the stratosphere but rather under their very feet—that Jesus' ascension did not remove his presence from earth but transformed it. Thus clued in, the disciples hastened to Jerusalem, which, in the Jewish mindset, was the center of the world. From there, they set to work transforming the world.

Like Roy, on some subconscious level, we followers of Jesus know that our ultimate destiny is connected with this earth. As a result, we are compelled not to build mashed-potato mountains but to build and renew the earth and all that is in it. And we do it in ways both profound and mundane. For example:

- We renew our physical selves by putting on makeup, fixing our hair, or just picking out the clothes we want to wear each day.
- We renew our spiritual selves by expressing ourselves through various forms of art.
- We renew our homes by planting gardens, tending our lawns, painting, wallpapering, and installing new carpets.

- We renew our communities by seeking improvements through elections, referendums, and civic projects.
- We renew our relationships by spending time with people, even—or especially—after we have encountered difficulties with them.

If our destiny lies elsewhere, why bother with all this earth-based renewal? If we're just going to leave it behind, why not let it rot and patiently wait for our ride to come? No, we do all these things for the same foggy but confident reason that Roy Neary built his mashed-potato mountain: we have this unshakable inkling that these things are important; that they mean something; and that they have something to do with our future—a future that has been shaped by the resurrection of Jesus Christ. This is precisely why St. Paul said, "For now we see in a mirror, dimly; but then we will see face to face. Now I know only in part; then I will know fully, even as I have been fully known" (1 Corinthians 13:12). As though peering into a hazy mirror, we perceive a not-so-clear image of a future that promises a renewed earth and renewed selves.

Where the Action Is

In 2013, the Rolling Stones launched their "50 and Counting" tour, playing shows at major venues in ten North American cities. But the Stones are also known for showing up unannounced at small music venues to play their brand of rock-and-roll for stunned and overjoyed audiences who just happen to be in the right place at the right time. Of course, not everyone is caught off guard. Many Stones fans anticipate where the band might show up and head to those spots in the hopes of being right. Indeed, those who know what the Stones are all about and have conformed themselves to the Stones' way of thinking about music are quite capable of guessing where the action might be.

As we Christians look to our future, it's important for us, too, to know where "the action" is going to be. Scripture makes it clear that "the action" will take place in an end time in which those who have conformed themselves to Christ will be "rewarded" with a renewed body and partner with him in caring for a renewed earth—a renewed creation. Consider the Memorial Acclamation, said during the Eucharist. In that prayer, we do not say, "When we eat this Bread and drink this Cup, we proclaim your Death, O Lord, *until we get to heaven*," but rather, "*until you come again*." This is where the action will be—right here on earth—but on a renewed earth completely joined with heaven. And because this is where the action *will be* in the future, it is also where the action *is*, or at least should be, in the present.

Matching Gifts

I love it when a company offers a "matching gift" program. This means that if you decide to make a charitable donation to a specific cause, the company will give an equal amount (or a percentage of it), thus increasing the magnitude of your initial act of charity. Such acts create a ripple effect. We are not directly rewarded for our act of charity, but we delight in the knowledge of the good it and the matching gift will do.

This is precisely why we Christians are called to do good works in the here and now—not so that we can earn an immediate personal reward, but so that our works will be multiplied by God when he renews creation at the end of time. We are not called simply to sit back and wait for "the world to come." Instead, we anticipate and begin to participate in the "world to come" through the good works we do now, knowing that they will somehow carry over and be magnified by God in the future. We seek to renew ourselves, our homes, our communities, our relationships, our environment, and our world in joyful anticipation of the day when God will renew them and us fully. In the meantime, we do these things because we have this unshakable inkling that they are important—they mean something.

Knowing that we have a God who is eager to "match" and magnify our good works as part of his plan to renew all of creation leads us to live as a people of the Resurrection: a people of hope. Sadly, this virtue is all too rare in our world. Therefore, to live as a person of hope is to behave in such a manner as to draw suspicion for violating worldly norms. Just as Roy Neary's strange behavior is shaped by a certain inkling that he is being drawn toward an ultimate destiny, so is ours shaped by a certain inkling that we are being drawn toward a new kind of living. This strange behavior—which, as you may recall, led people to conclude the apostles were drunk on Pentecost—is characterized by the following nine "tendencies," which we touched on briefly in chapter 1. Let's consider them more fully now.

Tendency 1: Putting one's own needs aside to tend to the needs of others

At the annual Christmas party at the school where I once taught, one of the veteran teachers who was usually quiet and reserved would drink a little too much and spend the rest of the evening hugging us all and saying how much he loved us. Once sobriety returned the next day, however, the love was gone. By contrast, the uninhibited love that flows in the kingdom of God as a result of the resurrection of Christ is not just a fleeting warm fuzzy feeling. It is an ongoing, unselfish concern for the good of others.

In fact, the better word here is *charity*—the kind of love God shows us and we can show others. This kind of love is totally selfless; it involves sacrifice because it means putting our own needs on the back burner. Those who bask in the glow of the resurrection of Christ and look forward to the resurrection of the body are known above all else for their selfless love. So much so that Tertullian, a second-century church father, reports that the Romans took special note of this characteristic when observing Christians. "See how they love one another," the Romans marveled. This doesn't mean that early Christians "love-bombed" one another with hugs and expressions of affection (although such displays did occur), but rather that they were known to act consistently not in their own interests but in the interests of others.

Tendency 2: Having a lightness of being and the ability to brighten up a room

Happiness and joy are not the same thing. Kingdom-dwellers are not people who put on rose-colored glasses and flippantly sing, "Don't worry; be happy!" No, kingdom-dwellers are filled with a deep and limitless joy, one that bears little resemblance to fleeting euphoria. This joy is a pervasive, abiding gladness, an inner peace that flows from being secure in God's love. And nothing makes us more joyful and secure than the knowledge that Jesus Christ is risen and will come again! As a result, joy is capable of withstanding anything that life tosses its way, even suffering.

The best example of joy that I ever came across was when I attended the wake of a friend's husband. As I offered my condolences and we chatted, my friend paused and said, "I'm filled with such joy right now." Of course she was not feeling happy; but she was experiencing a deep-down reassurance that everything was going to be okay because she recognized the presence of God and the promise of eternal life in the moment. Kingdom-dwellers like my friend can embrace joy because they know that death is not the end—and they learned this from the Resurrection.

Indeed, joy is at the very heart of the kingdom of God; and before we invite someone to enter the kingdom of God, we had better show some joy. In his book *Celebration of Discipline*, Richard Foster emphasizes the need for joy in the Christian life because "it is an occupational hazard of devout folk to become stuffy bores. They should not be. Of all people, we should be the most free, alive, interesting. Celebration adds a note of festivity and hilarity to our lives." While joy may not always be expressed in smiles and laughter, it *is* always characterized by a lack of cynicism and negativity. Joy leaves no room for despair. In one of his daily homilies, Pope Francis summed it up this way: "Long faces cannot proclaim Jesus. Joy alone and praise of God are the only way to advance the Gospel." This is why there are more feast days than fast days in the Christian calendar: joy trumps sorrow!

Tendency 3: Living in a state of serenity, even in the midst of turmoil

As a kid, I was particularly enamored with the following characters from TV and the movies: Sheriff Andy Taylor (*The Andy Griffith Show*), Glinda the Good Witch (*The Wizard of Oz*), and Underdog (voiced by Wally Cox). They shared one thing in common. They were unflappable. Sheriff Taylor didn't even need to carry a gun. Glinda was the only one who didn't cower when the Wicked Witch of the West appeared. And Underdog—well, "There's no need to fear. Underdog is here!" Need I say more?

I always wanted to have a similar sense of security, one that was unwavering. In Scripture, this is known as peace. Peace is what results when our will and the will of God correspond within the human heart. When we are anchored in God, we experience deep contentment and inner peace. Kingdom-dwellers anchored in the risen Christ are capable of navigating stormy waters without fear. In reality, every human being is grounded—centered—in God, who creates and sustains us. Unfortunately, our awareness of this groundedness fluctuates from day to day, especially in times of turmoil. And when we lose the awareness, we lose the peace and contentment. We become more like

Deputy Barney Fife, the Cowardly Lion, and Polly Purebred (Underdog's damsel in distress) than Sheriff Taylor, Glinda, or Underdog.

One of the best ways to maintain peace and contentment is prayer—especially contemplative prayer, which takes to heart the scriptural exhortation, "Be still, and know that I am God!" (Psalm 46:10). Prayer does not put us in a safety bubble that will prevent bad things from happening, but rather helps us to put our trust in God, who will uphold us through the moments of turmoil. In other words, we do not pray to escape reality but rather to remain in touch with a deeper reality. Likewise, prayer assists us in overcoming not only the external noise of our lives but also the internal chaos of our soul. Sitting in a quiet place does not ensure peace if our inner life is in turmoil. It helps us face our inner restlessness and find peace by learning to still our minds, bodies, and hearts and to anchor ourselves in God so that his will may be done on earth (in our hearts) as it is in heaven.

Tendency 4: Winking at the foibles and shortcomings of others instead of putting people in their place

When a lender and a borrower enter into an agreement to delay the foreclosure process, that agreement is called a forbearance. It basically means that the lender agrees to "hold back"—to be patient with the borrower until he or she can catch up on payments. When Jesus rose from the dead, he could have returned with a vengeance, seeking payment from all those who had betrayed, denied, and abandoned him. Instead, he brought forgiveness and reconciliation and called on the recipients of his mercy to do the same for others.

Kingdom-dwellers are called to practice this kind of forbearance in their relationships. This is not easy to do in a world that encourages us to give people their "just deserts"—the kind of response that Barabbas represents. To do otherwise is seen in the eyes of the world as weakness. To be truthful, it is not in our nature to do otherwise. The ability to love others in spite of their glaring weaknesses is a strength that comes to us from God: it certainly doesn't come from ourselves. It is easy to love those who love us. The gift of forbearance, however, enables us to love those who have wronged us. God himself models this kind of love in Scripture—in the New Testament in the person of Christ, of course, but often in the Old Testament, as well. Those who are under the impression that the Old Testament God is a vengeful one may be surprised to learn that on more than a dozen occasions, he is described as "slow to anger"—by the very people who had done something to provoke God's wrath.

As people made in God's image, we are called to respond similarly. Being slow to anger does *not* mean that we should behave like doormats, or worse, cultivate a "martyr complex" by letting everyone know how wronged and yet stoically nonreactive we have been. Rather, it means that we step out of the way and let God's love and justice filter through. Without forbearance, we become Barabbas: self-appointed judge, jury, and executioner, meting out justice as we see fit. Forbearance, on the other hand, gives us the perspective that enables us to love the sinner but hate the sin. It enables us to overcome self-pity and to avoid resentment and the desire for revenge.

Dr. Martin Luther King Jr. exhorted those fighting for civil rights to meet physical force with what he called "soul force." In other words, he urged them to endure wrongs patiently but not to cover them up or minimize them. Years before Martin Luther King arrived on the scene, Jackie Robinson practiced the same brand of forbearance. He got out of the way and let the abuse he experienced speak for itself. Ultimately, he allowed God's judgment to take its course, and history was transformed.

Forgiving someone seventy times seven times is not a recipe for the weak. It takes strength to endure the wrong itself, but also to trust that the wrong will be dealt with and transformed by God's justice, in God's time.

Tendency 5: Responding to even the grumpiest of people with graciousness and civility

The most-dreaded word when it comes to medical diagnoses is *malignant*. When a tumor is found to be malignant, it means that its purpose is to destroy. The opposite of something malignant, then, is something whose purpose is to build up and do good. For some reason, however, the word *benign—malignant's* antonym—has come to mean little more than "neutral." A benign tumor, for example, is typically removed: it might not be causing harm, but it's not doing any good, either.

Let's shift our thinking about the word *benign* and restore its original meaning: To be *benign* is to be kind and to actively do good. (The two are related, of course, since kindness is shown through actions.) As a result of Christ's resurrection, kingdom-dwellers are prone to kindness—to acts that are intrinsically good. Grandparents are the best examples of this type of kindness. They can't wait to be with their grandchildren so they can spoil them with goodness and then send them on their way. I was told many years ago that a loving grandparent is the closest thing we have on this earth to an experience of God—and ain't it the truth? Such unlimited generosity speaks to us (if we let it) of the presence of God, whom, the church teaches, is "absolute benignity." In other words, it is God's very nature to heap blessings on his children. This nature is shown time and again in Scripture, culminating in the blessing of the resurrection of Christ. Under the influence of the risen Christ, we are compelled to do the same for others, actively and generously spreading kindness—benignity—rather than malignancy.

Tendency 6: Keeping the best interests of others in mind, even when they fail us

In the movie *Cool Hand Luke*, the captain of the chain gang tells Luke, a prisoner (played by Paul Newman), that wearing those chains is "for your own good," to which Luke replies, "Wish you'd stop bein' so good to me, cap'n." Luke recognizes that the word *good* is thrown around so much that it often means nothing. He certainly knew that the captain didn't have his best interests in mind. In Scripture, goodness is more than mere amiability. It is an attribute of God manifested by his constant attention to humankind's best interests, even when humankind repeatedly fails. No one would ever think to say, "I wish you'd stop bein' so good to me, God," because God's goodness *is* to our benefit.

As a result of the resurrection of Jesus Christ, kingdom-dwellers bring that goodness of God to others—always with their best interests in mind. Goodness is not measured by one's ability to avoid doing bad things. Rather, it is an active trait, an almost compulsive desire to pursue the best interests of others, often at the cost of one's own needs. George Bailey in *It's a Wonderful Life* comes to mind. George is someone who continually puts his own dreams on the back burner in order to enable someone else to achieve theirs. That's what it means to be a martyr—not in the "Woe is me" sense, but in the sense of putting one's own life aside for others.

To lay down one's life does not necessarily mean to physically die but to set aside your own needs to tend to the needs of others. Parents and spouses do this each and every day, which is why marriage and parenthood can be two of the most significant conversion experiences in a person's life. But anyone who unselfishly and sincerely provides a service to others, with or without monetary compensation, is participating in goodness: teachers, first responders, customer-service representatives, medical personnel, hairdressers, flight attendants, and so on. No matter how trying the situation in which they find themselves, kingdom-dwellers make a habit of keeping the best interests of others in mind.

Tendency 7: Staying on message, even under duress

"Oh, to hell with it." That's an interesting phrase. We use it when we feel like quitting—like giving up. We use it when we don't feel like it's worth giving a particular task our best effort. So why do we send the task to *hell*? Probably because hell is thought to be a "place" devoid of hope. What we're saying when we say "to hell with it" is that we ourselves feel trapped in hopelessness.

And yet even though life is full of challenges and obstacles that can lead to despair, there are some folks who never give up. No matter how dire the circumstances, they stay focused and positive; they continue to believe that the task at hand will bear fruit. A brilliantly hilarious example of this never-say-die attitude is portrayed in the classic comedy film *Monty Python and the Holy Grail*. When King Arthur (played by Graham Chapman) encounters the fearsome Black Knight (played by John Cleese) and commands him to step aside, the Black Knight refuses. The two men draw their swords, and after a short skirmish, King Arthur chops off the Black Knight's left arm. With good reason, the king assumes the knight will then step aside and allow him to pass. But no. The Black Knight insists that his wound is simply a scratch and that he's "had worse."

The battle resumes, and this time, Arthur chops off the Black Knight's *right* arm. Much to Arthur's amazement, the Black Knight will not relent and continues to taunt Arthur and stand in his way, referring to his loss of limbs as "just a flesh wound." Despite the loss of both arms, the Black Knight prolongs the battle by kicking Arthur, who responds by chopping off first one of the Black Knight's legs and then the other. Finally free to pass, Arthur does so, but still the

Black Knight persists. "Oh, oh, I see," he shouts. "Running away then. Come back here and take what's coming to you. I'll bite your legs off!"

Now *that's* staying on mission! Of course, *Monty Python* is a fictional comedy. What about in real life? Perhaps the best example I ever encountered of real-world tenacity was in the person of Fr. Larry Craig, who did prison ministry for many years in Chicago before his untimely death in 2006. Once, when I took a group of Catholic high school students to visit him, a student asked how many lives he had "turned around" in his work. Fr. Craig said, "Let's see. I've been doing this for fifteen years . . . worked with about 5,000 inmates . . . probably reached six of them. Next question." I interrupted and asked him how he was able to motivate himself, given such a low "success rate." He replied, "I do it because it's the right thing to do. Jesus said 'when I was in prison you visited me.' Next question." Now *that's* staying on mission in the real world—and in the kingdom of God.

Tendency 8: Remaining even-keeled and reasonable in the face of conflict

We don't use the word *meek* too often nowadays. The only time I can remember hearing this word as a kid (other than in the "Blessed are the meek" Beatitude) was in the *Wizard of Oz*, when Dorothy introduces herself to Oz, the great and powerful, as "Dorothy, the small and meek." Naturally, I grew up thinking that to be meek was to be the opposite of powerful: weak and powerless. If I had been looking for someone to go up against the great and powerful Oz, I'd have picked Barabbas over Dorothy any day.

Surprisingly though, there is also a popular saying that goes, "If you think meek is weak, try being meek for a week." In Scripture, meekness is not weakness and has no affinity for cowards. Rather, it is a quiet strength acquired through self-discipline. If meekness were an NHL hockey player, it would receive the Lady Byng Memorial Trophy—an award bestowed upon the player who combines sportsmanship and gentlemanly conduct with excellence in the game. Among NHL greats who have won this trophy are Wayne Gretzky, Bobby Hull, Stan Mikita, Pavel Datsyuk, Alex Delvecchio, and Mike Bossy—and if you know anything about any of these players, you wouldn't dare call them weak. But they did indeed embody the scriptural quality of meekness in their approach to the game. They could take a hit, even a dirty one, and just keep on playing their game instead of retaliating and ending up in the penalty box along with the goon who roughed them up in the first place.

Unfortunately, since Jesus is described as "meek" in the Gospels (see, for example, Matthew 21:5), we often see him depicted in art as looking weak. And not just weak—he too often looks like a wimp. But Jesus was certainly no wimp. As a carpenter, he would be the equivalent of a modern-day construction worker, hard-hat and all. And when he calls himself the "good shepherd" (John 10:11), we need to recall that in those days a shepherd was the equivalent of a cowboy. Jesus stood toe-to-toe with the most powerful men in society and never backed down. Even as he faced the abuse and taunts of his executioners, he did not cower, nor did he strike back. Rather, he absorbed their most ferocious blows, patiently trusting that God had something greater planned for him.

Smart hockey players will tell you that the best way to give payback for a cheap hit is to score a goal and win the game rather than respond with a cheap shot of your own. This type of meekness—disciplined, harnessed strength—allows one to strive for something greater instead of settle for a petty response. One who remains meek is able to see and think clearly, and as a result, is able to reach for higher things. Meekness is at the heart of the saying "Choose your battles wisely." Because of the resurrection of Jesus, we are able to absorb the blows that life sends our way, knowing that we have a greater weapon and a greater goal than vengeance.

Tendency 9: Practicing mindfulness

Try signing your name with your nondominant hand. Unless you're ambidextrous, this is not easy. What we typically do mindlessly now requires effort. Anyone who has lost the use of a limb, whether temporarily or permanently, can attest to the amount of effort it takes to adjust to using either the other limb or a prosthesis. Experts tell us that when patients are recovering from an amputation, they go through several steps: numbness, pining for what is lost, and finally disorganization (or despair) before reaching what is called *reorganization,* or a new way of thinking and living. Before reaching reorganization, however, many amputees experience a phenomenon known as "phantom limb sensation"—the sensation that the lost limb is still present and active.

New habits require mindfulness because old habits are like lost limbs: even when they are "gone," they continue to demand attention. In their book *Savor: Mindful Eating, Mindful Life*, Thich Nhat Hanh and Dr. Lilian Cheung talk about the importance of mindfulness when developing new habits. They tell a classic Zen story of a man riding a galloping horse, which gives the impression of an important, urgent quest. However, when a bystander asks where he is going, the rider responds, "I don't know! Ask the horse!" In other words (as we discussed in the last chapter), a certain degree of mindfulness is required to avoid riding slipshod through life on the backs of our runaway habits. When St. Paul speaks about living under the influence of the risen Christ (what he calls "life in the Spirit"), he emphasizes that only a new mindfulness can break the mindless old habits of sin (what he calls "life in the flesh").

> For those who live according to the flesh *set their minds* on the
> things of the flesh, but those who live according to the Spirit *set*
> *their minds* on the things of the Spirit. To *set the mind* on the flesh
> is death, but to set the mind on the Spirit is life and peace.
>
> — Romans 8:5–6 (emphases mine)

Paul goes on to describe how mindfulness is like living in the light,
while our old habits—mindlessness—are like living in darkness:

> Let us then lay aside the works of darkness and put on the armor of
> light; let us live honorably as in the day, not in reveling and drunk-
> enness, not in debauchery and licentiousness, not in quarreling and
> jealousy. Instead, put on the Lord Jesus Christ, and make no provi-
> sion for the flesh, to gratify its desires.
>
> —Romans 13:12–14

"Life in the Spirit" requires a "reorganization" in order to leave behind
"life in the flesh"—much as an amputee requires reorganization to overcome "phantom limb sensation." "Life in the flesh" is life that is mindless, rooted in patterns of behavior that our naturally self-centered brain
dictates. "Life in the Spirit," on the other hand, requires a mindfulness
that shifts the focus away from the self and onto others. This does not
come naturally to us and requires work. It's like learning to live with a
prosthesis after an amputation: ongoing therapy is needed so that the
individual can see himself or herself as a "new me." Similarly, it is only
through mindfulness that an idea becomes a belief and a belief is manifested in action. Kingdom-dwelling requires constant "therapy" so that
we can repent (in Hebrew, *metanoia,* which means to "go beyond the
mind that you have") and become a new creation.

> So whoever is in Christ is a new creation: the old things have passed
> away; behold, new things have come.
>
> —2 Corinthians 5:17, NAB

Fruit Is Good for You

If any of the nine behaviors discussed above sound slightly familiar to you, they should be: Christians traditionally refer to them as the "fruits of the spirit," which come to us from St. Paul:

> By contrast, the fruit of the Spirit is love, joy, peace, patience, kindness, generosity, faithfulness, gentleness, and self-control.
>
> —Galatians 5:22–23

In my book *7 Keys to Spiritual Wellness*, I "repackaged" the "seven deadly sins"; here, I have similarly repackaged the nine fruits of the spirit, known traditionally as the following:

- love (putting one's own needs aside to tend to the needs of others)
- joy (having lightness of being and the ability to brighten up a room)
- peace (living in a state of serenity, even in the midst of turmoil)
- patience (winking at the foibles and shortcomings of others instead of putting people in their place)
- kindness (responding to even the grumpiest of people with graciousness and civility)
- generosity (keeping the best interests of others in mind, even when they fail us)
- faithfulness (staying on message, even under duress)
- gentleness (remaining even keeled and reasonable in the face of conflict)
- self-control (practicing mindfulness)

The early Christians, thoroughly intoxicated with the spirit of the risen Christ, embodied these behaviors and lived them in a contagious way. This tells us that the roots of effective evangelization are not primarily words but rather behaviors. As a young atheist once said, "Christianity is something that if you *really* believed it, it would change your life and you would want to change [the lives] of others. I haven't seen too much of that." The fruits of the spirit can and must be seen in the life of anyone who professes faith in the resurrection of Christ.

Living with Hope

The bottom line is this: the resurrection of Jesus Christ enables us to live in confident hope, knowing that we have a future that includes a renewed body living on a renewed earth within a renewed cosmos. People who live in this confident hope have a giddiness that is contagious. Today, we live in a world that too often tempts us to despair. To be a follower of the risen Christ is to take confident hope (because the promise comes from a reliable source—the risen Christ) into places of despair so that life may be transformed and have meaning. Christian hope recognizes and acknowledges pain and suffering (the perceived absence of God) but believes in a future that overflows into the present with the presence of God. When our present is filled with pain and suffering, we become insecure and preoccupied with self-preservation. Such insecurity causes us to be fearful, anxious, and greedy—all qualities that force us to operate out of a narrow space (the *pusilla anima,* or small soul) and prevent us from truly loving others. Hope, on the other hand, embraces the promise of security, which in turn expands the soul (*magna anima,* or great soul) and breeds selfless love—the kind of love that reveals the face of God. Christian hope is buoyed by the seeds of a new world already taking shape in this life. It is a hope that energizes us to live differently and compels us to spread the word that life is indeed worth living.

Armed with the new life of the risen Christ, we are ready to forge ahead and pitch our tent in the new reality known as the kingdom of God. Let's turn now to the invitation extended to us by the risen Christ: the invitation to change our spiritual zip code.

6

Are You out of Your Mind?

The Invitation to Follow Jesus

Follow me, and I will make you fishers of men.
—Matthew 4:19, AV

On the Web site of the Make-A-Wish Foundation, you can find heart-warming stories about children suffering from life-threatening medical conditions enjoying a dream-come-true through the efforts of that foundation. You can learn about Brandon, who was battling a renal disorder at the age of seven and wished to be a firefighter. Or fifteen-year-old Hanna, who suffered from Ewing's sarcoma and wanted nothing other than to perform with the Chicago Symphony Orchestra. Or nine-year-old Ty, who was dealing with muscular dystrophy and dreamed of playing for the San Francisco 49ers. What's special about the Make-A-Wish Foundation is that it doesn't just place the child *close* to his or her dream to admire it from the sidelines; it puts the child *inside* the dream to experience it in full. Brandon received his fireman's uniform and helmet, was flown on a helicopter, and then rode with the company of firefighters to put out a car fire. Hanna not only attended a performance of the Chicago Symphony Orchestra and met the musicians, but she actually got to play with the French-horn section. Ty signed a short-term contract, got his own locker and uniform, and went onto the field with his gridiron heroes.

Jesus works the same way. He doesn't invite us simply to get close to God and admire him from nearby. He invites us to enter into the very life of God—the Trinity—and to experience it as fully as we humans are able. The invitation to live the Christian life is not to stand outside of God's kingdom, throwing pebbles at the windows to get God's attention and maybe, if we're lucky, to talk to him from a distance. Rather, it is an invitation into communion with God. It is an invitation to experience the divine life firsthand.

It's a golden invitation.

Everybody loves a golden invitation. From the time we were kids, choosing up sides for a ball game, we desired to be selected in an early round by the older kid we admired and wanted to be like. We longed to be asked out on a date by the guy or girl of our dreams. We hoped to be pursued by the corporation or firm that would give us an opportunity to shine at our dream job. The thrill of unexpectedly receiving a golden invitation is captured in the classic Bruce Springsteen music video for *Dancing in the Dark*: an adoring front-row fan (played by the twenty-year-old Courtney Cox) beams with excitement and delight when Bruce chooses her to jump up on stage and dance with him. Enjoying the show from the first row is one thing. Being pulled up on stage to dance with The Boss is another.

To admire Jesus from a distance is to misunderstand what he desires of us. Ultimately, Jesus is not to be admired from a distance: he is to be known on an intimate basis. Jesus does not ask Peter, "Do you have sufficient knowledge of all that I have said and done?" but rather, "Do you love me?"—a question that probes the deepest connection between human beings. Jesus does not desire *fans* who cheer from the sidelines but rather *friends* who will roll up their sleeves and work shoulder to shoulder with him to build the kingdom of

God. To truly encounter Christ is to experience another way of being human—viewing life from within the mind of Christ.

Christ, What Are You Thinking?

Imagine that a young person dealing with a life-threatening illness approaches the Make-A-Wish Foundation and says that his or her wish is to spend a day as a disciple of Jesus Christ. What would such a day look like? It would certainly involve more than simply reading some literature about Jesus. To be a disciple of Christ requires more than an intellectual acknowledgment of God's existence. It means more than accumulating knowledge about Jesus. Rather, it is an experience of friendship with God. It is an experience of getting out of our minds so that, as St. Paul wrote, we may "have the mind of Christ" (1 Corinthians 2:16).

To "have the mind of Christ" is to align our spiritual lives with the inner life of Christ as closely as possible. To do this, we must first ask Christ, "What are you thinking?" Luckily for us, we need not be mind readers; Jesus Christ did not keep his thoughts secret. In fact, quite the opposite. Throughout all of salvation history, God goes out of his way to reveal his mind to us, and this revelation is completed in Christ. Christian discipleship, then, refers to our efforts to "map" the mind of Christ and to live within it and operate out of it as spirituality. Those who do this best are called saints. They were out of their minds—and into the mind of Christ.

One such saint was Ignatius of Loyola, the founder of the Society of Jesus. Ignatius was doing the work of the Make-A-Wish Foundation centuries before that organization was born. Just as Make-A-Wish enables young people dealing with physical threats to immerse themselves in experiences they have always dreamed of, Ignatius enabled people of all ages dealing with spiritual threats to immerse themselves in the mind of Christ. He was so good at it, in fact, that the practice of "mapping" the mind of Christ is now referred to as Ignatian spirituality. In essence, when Ignatius invites us to become a disciple of Christ—to put on the mind of Christ—he invites us to

- awaken our deepest desires;
- develop an awareness of our own desirability in God's eyes;
- experience God's nearness;
- deepen our desire to be actively involved in God's work;
- experience intimacy with God;
- stop trying to save ourselves;
- seek out others with whom to share the journey;
- allow God to color our world;
- profoundly revere each person as he or she is;
- give thanks;
- live as a person for others; and
- navigate through the gray areas of life.

If the Make-A-Wish Foundation planned for each of us to spend a day as a disciple of Jesus, each of those days would look different. Your day would match your location in life and your own unique gifts, just as my day would match mine. However, the twelve components listed above would be the desired outcomes for all people wishing to get out of their own mind and into the mind of Christ. In many ways, these twelve outcomes are like the twelve baskets of leftovers after Jesus fed the five thousand (see Matthew 14:20): they originate with Jesus' generosity, they nourish us fully, and they expand outward from us to others. Let's take a closer look at each of these baskets of abundance of which we are being invited to partake.

Basket 1: Discipleship Invites Us to Awaken Our Deepest Desires

It's always fun when the lottery jackpot grows to enormous proportions and ticket buyers begin to speculate about what they would do with their winnings. If you've not already engaged in such speculation yourself, you should try it. The exercise tends to put us in touch with our deepest desires. And contrary to popular thought, following Jesus does not require the repression of all desires. Instead, discipleship not only awakens our deepest desires but also reveals them to be pale imitations of the even deeper desire to transcend ourselves and experience the divine. As the *Catechism of the Catholic Church* reminds us, "the desire for God is written in the human heart" (27); and as Jesus himself teaches, "Where your treasure is, there your heart will be also" (Matthew 6:21).

The question is, what do you treasure most? What is your life centered on?

Jesus himself was tempted during his forty days in the desert to center his life on pleasure, power, and possessions, but he instead chose to center his life on God—and he invites us to do the same. He invites us to take pleasure in God, to rely on his power, and to possess his kingdom. To help us stay centered on God, disciples of Jesus use certain symbolic strategies. We practice fasting, on occasion, to remind us that our ultimate pleasure is found in God. We practice prayer to tap into the power of God instead of relying only on ourselves. We practice almsgiving to remind ourselves that possessing the kingdom is more important than possessing material goods. We don't do these things to squelch our desires but rather to awaken them and channel them toward God, who alone satisfies the hungry heart. As St. Augustine said, "Our hearts are restless, Lord, until they rest in you." Or, put another way, "our desires remain unfulfilled, Lord, until they are fulfilled in you."

Basket 2: Discipleship Invites Us to a Deeper Awareness of Our Own Desirability in God's Eyes

Do you know what it's like to have a secret admirer? I remember once, when I was a teenager, I was playing in a hockey game in a gym at the Boys' Club when I collided with another player. I flew up in the air, did a somersault, and landed on my back. While I was somersaulting through the air, seemingly in slow motion, I heard a girl's voice from the bleachers cry out with concern, "Joey!" When I landed, I looked about, but was unable to spot anyone who may have called my name. I got up and played the rest of that game with a renewed fervor, knowing there was a girl in the stands who seemed interested in me—a new phenomenon in my life! I never did find out who had called my name, but the very notion that someone might be interested in me had awakened something deep inside.

Too many people go through life thinking they are undesirable in the eyes of others and even in the eyes of God. Discipleship, on the other hand, invites us to realize that we are infinitely desirable in the eyes of God, who has a unique love for each of us. When Jesus was baptized, a voice from heaven was heard to say, "This is my Son, the Beloved, with whom I am well pleased" (Matthew 3:17). These words speak not only of Jesus, but also of those to whom he was sent. God must love us immeasurably to have sent his only Son to become one of us. This is precisely the point of the well-known Gospel passage John 3:16: "For God so loved the world that he gave his only Son, so that everyone who believes in him may not perish but may have eternal life." Discipleship awakens within us the notion that God is uniquely interested in each of us. So much so that Jesus reminds us, "You did not choose me but I chose you" (John 15:16). It is always nice to know that someone desires us, especially when that person is someone we ourselves desire!

Basket 3: Discipleship Invites Us to Experience God's Nearness

When I was a teenager, I often spent time at my friend Casey's house. His dad, who enjoyed having guests in his home, was always eager to share his favorite line of advice whenever he got the chance. "Joey," he would say, "stay close to God!" I wonder if he knew how Ignatian he was. St. Ignatius taught that discipleship—having the mind of Christ—is "powered" by the realization and experience of God's nearness. At the heart of Christianity is the belief that God became one with us through the birth of his Son, Jesus Christ. We call this the Incarnation. We believe that God is not distant, but rather is intimately involved with us, creating us moment by moment. You may think that even Jesus doubted the nearness of his Father when he cried out from the cross, "My God, my God, why have you forsaken me?" (Matthew 27:46). With these words, Jesus was praying Psalm 22, which continues as follows:

> Yet it was you who took me from the womb;
> > you kept me safe on my mother's breast.
> On you I was cast from my birth,
> > and since my mother bore me you have been my God.
> Do not be far from me,
> > for trouble is near
> > and there is no one to help.

> —Psalm 22:9–11

After several additional appeals for help, the psalm builds toward a confident proclamation in the nearness of God: "he did not hide his face from me, / but heard when I cried to him" (Psalm 22:24). In praying this psalm on the cross, then, Jesus was not only calling for his Father's help but also reminding himself and us that his Father was near. Later, before he ascended, Jesus would assure the disciples of his own nearness as they went forth to continue his mission: "And remember," he told them, "I am with you always, to the end of the age" (Matthew 28:20).

To live as a disciple of Christ, then, is to live in the spirit of Psalm 139, knowing that Christ is near:

> Where can I go from your Spirit?
>> Or where can I flee from your presence?
> If I ascend to the heaven, you are there;
>> if I make my bed in Sheol, you are there.
> If I take the wings of the morning,
>> and settle at the farthest limits of the sea,
> even there your hand shall lead me,
>> and your right hand shall hold me fast.

—Psalm 139:7–10

Basket 4: Discipleship Invites Us to Deepen Our Desire to Be Actively Involved in God's Work

Every year, countless numbers of men shell out thousands of dollars to participate in baseball fantasy camps where they have the opportunity to play alongside some of the baseball greats they once looked up to as boys. The idea of encountering their former heroes and joining them in the game they love is a dream-come-true. Of course, the ultimate baseball-dream-come-true scenario takes place in the great movie *Field of Dreams*, when Ray Kinsella (played by Kevin Costner) is given a second chance to encounter his late father—a former baseball player—and to repair the strained relationship they shared in life. Who doesn't get choked up at the end of the movie when Ray calls out to his father, John Kinsella, "Hey Dad? You wanna have a catch?" As we dab our tears, the two of them wordlessly toss a baseball back and forth. Their relationship is healed through a simple encounter on a baseball diamond.

Discipleship is our opportunity to encounter Jesus—to join him in "his game" and to walk and work alongside him. It is not just an opportunity to learn about Jesus Christ, but to encounter him and share experiences with him. Jesus assures us of this: " Those who love me will keep my word, and my Father will love them, and we will come to them and make our home with them" (John 14:23). When people live with you—make their home with you—you can't avoid a true encounter!

It turns out that in some fantasy baseball camps, few participants actually encounter the big-name ballplayer whose name appears on the camp literature. In discipleship, you not only shake hands with the Lord, you bunk with him. He will personally apprentice you day and night for the rest of your life.

Basket 5: Discipleship Invites Us to Experience Intimacy with God

When my daughter was a freshman at a Catholic high school, she had to prepare a prayer for religion class but seemed to be having trouble getting started. As we talked about it, I realized that she felt she had to "compose" a prayer as though God could only be approached through formal language. But St. Ignatius taught that when we pray, it should "resemble one friend speaking to another"—and I told her this. She was able to move forward, knowing that God was approachable in this manner.

The notion of speaking to God as a friend has deep roots in the Jewish faith: only a friend could say some of the things said to God in the psalms and get away with it! Similarly, in the great film *Fiddler on the Roof*, the title character, Tevye, constantly talks to God as a friend, covering topics that include his horse, his wife, his five daughters, the political climate, his lack of income, and, of course, his faith. And yet the idea of talking to God as a friend is either surprising or foreign to many Catholics—even though Jesus says to us, "I do not call you servants any longer, because the servant does not know what the master is doing; but I have called you friends, because I have made known to you everything that I have heard from my Father" (John 15:15). That's what intimate friends do: they share intimate thoughts and ideas.

Jesus reinforced this notion about the approachability of God when he taught his disciples to pray by addressing God as "Father." As I mentioned earlier, the term that Jesus used—*Abba*—is the equivalent of "papa," which is a term of endearment and affection used by children who feel close to their father. Our God is a relater: Father, Son, and Holy Spirit are in such an intimate relationship, they are one. And as people made in God's image, we are called, through discipleship, to intimacy with God and his children, our brothers and sisters. Can you relate?

Basket 6: Discipleship Invites Us to Stop Trying to Save Ourselves

If you located this book in the "Self-Help" section of a bookstore, you should immediately find the store manager and complain, because this book is the opposite of a self-help book. In fact, the very essence of Christianity is the antithesis of self-help: we gain access to the kingdom of God not through our own efforts but through the Person of Jesus Christ. This is a book about dependency. Healthy dependency.

Contrary to popular opinion, *dependency* is not a dirty word. We are dependent on others for many things. In fact, the most profound lesson in life may be the realization that, at our deepest level, we are incapable of sustaining ourselves. In their book *Healthy Dependency: Leaning on Others Without Losing Yourself,* authors Robert F. Bornstein, PhD, and Mary A. Languirand, PhD, explain that our culture teaches us not how to reconnect but how to disconnect. Their conclusion is that "to live life to its fullest, each of us must recapture the healthy dependency that exists within us."

Discipleship is an invitation to embrace the healthiest dependency there is: our dependency on our Creator through the Person who makes God accessible and visible, Jesus Christ. Discipleship is all about following—and the only reason we would ever follow someone is if we were dependent on him or her for something. (Think about following someone in a car through a strange city to a place whose location you are unfamiliar with.) This takes trust and vulnerability, the opposite of which is self-righteousness. Jesus makes it clear that self-righteousness is an obstacle to grace in his exchange with the Pharisees, whom he accused of being self-righteous, after he healed a man born blind:

> Jesus said, "I came into this world for judgment so that those who do not see may see, and those who see may become blind." Some of the Pharisees near him heard this and said to him, "Surely we are not blind, are we?" Jesus said to them, "If you were blind, you would not have sin. But now that you say, 'We see,' your sin remains."
>
> —John 9:39–41

Likewise, in the Genesis story of the fall of man, self-reliance is described as a kind of "seeing." The serpent tempted Adam and Eve with the notion of becoming all-seeing, all-powerful gods: "for God knows that when you eat of it your eyes will be opened, and you will be like God" (Genesis 3:5). In seeing all things, they believed, they would no longer need God, and so would have "saved" themselves.

But Jesus uses images not of independence but of dependence to illustrate our relationship with him:

- "I am the vine, you are the branches" (John 15:5).
- "I am the good shepherd" (John 10:14).

- "I am the way, and the truth, and the life" (John 14:6).

- "I have come to call not the righteous but sinners to repentance" (Luke 5:32).

- "Those who are well have no need of a physician, but those who are sick" (Mark 2:17).

Original sin is the mistaken notion that we can have perfect health and perfect vision without God—that we can save ourselves. Discipleship, on the other hand, is a way of life that embraces our basic blindness and imperfection and our need to be saved by Jesus Christ.

Basket 7: Discipleship Invites Us to Seek Out Others with Whom to Share the Journey

"Never again!" These words are often spoken by people who have experienced a failed relationship. And yet, after a period of healing, many of those same folks feel compelled to give relationships another try. The fact is, we human beings have a built-in desire for connectedness, but we also live in a culture that promotes individualism. As a result, loneliness is on the rise. According to University of Chicago social neuroscientist John Cacioppo, "It's not the number of relationships; it really is the quality of those relationships that determines whether you feel socially isolated." We may all have more "friends" these days, but not many of them know us deeply; and as a result, we feel loneliness more acutely.

Discipleship is the perfect remedy for isolation because Jesus is the ultimate gatherer. It is no accident that when Jesus sent out his disciples, he sent them out in pairs (see Mark 6:7). Discipleship is all about making connections. In fact, to be a disciple is to be a discipl*er*: one who makes other disciples. And when it came to discipling, Jesus invested his time and energy in groups of people, whether they were the seventy (see Luke 10), the twelve, or the three (Peter, James, and

John). Christianity, by its very nature, is a communal reality: love of God and love of neighbor are inseparable.

Increasingly in our culture today, people describe themselves as "spiritual" but "not religious." In large part, this trend can be attributed to the desire to have a relationship with the divine in isolation or at least apart from anything that smacks of ecclesial life—the life of the church. But in fact, a relationship with the divine in isolation is impossible. As I was writing this book, the great Chicago priest Fr. Andrew Greeley passed away. Fr. Greeley once commented, "If you can find a perfect church, go ahead and join it; but as soon as you do, it won't be perfect anymore." So true! Discipleship, by necessity, brings us into connection with others, warts and all, and with the notion that our salvation will not be found in isolation. This is precisely why the New Testament teaches that "those who say, 'I love God,' and hate their brothers or sisters, are liars; for those who do not love a brother or sister whom they have seen, cannot love God whom they have not seen" (1 John 4:20). Those who claim to be spiritual but not religious run the risk of exalting themselves ("I'm better than those involved in institutional religion"), while discipleship demands of us that we humble ourselves enough to associate with the "imperfect"—and even to wash their feet.

Basket 8: Discipleship Invites Us to Allow God to Color Our World

Try this experiment. Draw a pie chart of your life, creating slices for the following areas of attention: eating, sleeping, exercising, spending time with family, working, commuting, doing chores, recreating, and spending time with God. If you're like most people, this last slice will be embarrassingly small. Why? Because we tend to base it on the amount of time we spend at church or in prayer. To be more spiritual, we think, we need to spend more time in worship. But worship is only a small part of spirituality. True spirituality is the ability to see the whole pie—every slice of our life—as happening "in God." Discipleship colors our world so that we come to recognize God in all things and in all aspects of our lives. (This was the kind of vision Adam and Eve really needed—and, ironically, had, before the serpent came along.)

Do you remember what it was like the first time you fell in love? Suddenly, you looked at the world and all of life in a whole new way. The love that you were experiencing "colored" your entire world: it permeated and transformed every nook and cranny of your life. I, for one, remember sitting in trigonometry—a class I hated—with a big smile on my face, thinking about the girl I was falling in love with. Discipleship has a similar effect. It doesn't necessarily mean spending more time at church. Rather, it means seeing, sensing, and recognizing God in all the nooks and crannies of our lives—and smiling in spirit at the very thought.

This is what lies at the heart of the Gospel story of Martha and Mary (see Luke 10:38–42), a story often misunderstood as a lesson in achieving balance between action (Martha) and contemplation (Mary). In reality, this story is about Mary allowing Jesus to color her world. When Martha complains that she has too much work to do, Jesus responds on a different level: "You are worried and distracted by many things," he says, but "there is need of only one thing." If Jesus had told Martha to forget about the pots and pans and take a seat at his feet, she would *still* be distracted; she would still miss the fact that God was in their midst. Mary, on the other hand, had discovered the "one thing" needed: Jesus. Because of this, she could have gotten up to scrub those same pots and pans, but would have done so with peace and serenity, her heart still focused on him.

This notion of the "one thing" played a prominent role in the movie *City Slickers*, when Mitch (played by Billy Crystal) finds himself alone with the rugged cowboy known as Curly (played by the late Jack Palance). Holding up one finger, Curly reveals to Mitch that the secret of life comes down to "one thing." When Mitch presses him to reveal what that one thing is, Curly replies, "That's what you have to find out."

Discipleship enables us to find out the "one thing" needed: the love of God in Christ Jesus that colors our world—every nook and cranny of it. When this happens, we find ourselves finding God in all things.

Basket 9: Discipleship Invites Us to Profoundly Revere Each Person as He or She Is

Sad but true: some of the most detestable, inflammatory, and unchari-table rhetoric can be found in the comments sections of Christian Web sites and blogs. In our rush to lay claim to the truth, many of us Chris-tians are more than happy to cast nasty aspersions on those who do not share our views.

I recall once speaking to a group of parents at a Catholic parish, helping them to prepare for their children's First Holy Communion. In the Q & A that followed, one of the moms explained that she had just recently returned to the church after being away for some time, but that she was still having difficulty with certain issues, among them, the prohibition against women priests. I sought to be very pastoral in my response, telling her that I understood how this issue might be a stumbling block. I felt my role at that moment was to continue to nurture her return to the faith, especially as her child was preparing to meet Jesus in the Eucharist. The next day, I received a nasty e-mail from a gentleman who had been in attendance the previous night. In it, he accused me of being cowardly in not articulating the church's teaching on this matter, which is that the topic is closed to discussion. He also claimed that he could conclude what my answers to ques-tions about abortion, artificial contraception, and gay marriage would be. He, of course, was entitled to object to my approach to the first issue; however, in his haste to gain the moral high ground, he did what too many of us Christians are doing these days at an alarming rate: he rushed to judgment, which, as you may recall, is a violation of the eighth commandment: "You shall not bear false witness against your neighbor." This commandment is not just about telling lies; it is about respecting the truth. The *Catechism of the Catholic Church* explicitly states that we are guilty of breaking the eighth commandment when we rush to judgment and assume as true "without sufficient foundation, the moral fault of a neighbor" (2477). The *Catechism* goes on to say that we can avoid this pitfall by carefully considering "insofar as possible [our] neighbor's thoughts, words, and deeds in a favorable way" (2478).

Jesus taught his disciples and he teaches us that we will encounter difficult audiences in our quest to spread the Good News. He makes it very clear, however, that if "anyone will not welcome you or listen to your words, shake off the dust from your feet as you leave that house or town" (Matthew 10:14). Jesus does not suggest that we call them idiots. To encounter Jesus is to encounter the truth—"I am the way, and the truth, and the life" (John 14:6)—but this does not make everyone else false.

I have a daily calendar on my desk with cartoons by Doug Hall (many of which appear in my previous books, *The Catechist's Toolbox*, *The Bible Blueprint*, *A Well-Built Faith*, and *Practice Makes Catholic*). One of these cartoons depicts a pastor preaching to a completely empty church and exclaiming, "We have achieved our goal of complete moral purity." This is hilarious, but also sad, since some contemporary Christians actively express the opinion that what we need is a "smaller but purer" church. But can you imagine trying that line on the Jesus who dined with tax collectors, prostitutes, and sinners? Jesus isn't interested in a smaller, purer church. On the contrary, when describing how the kingdom will grow, he uses the imagery of casting a dragnet and allowing the wheat and the weeds to grow together. We'll be fine as disciples of Christ as long as we are faithful to the truth—and that means having respect for and patience with those who are not quite there yet.

Basket 10: Discipleship Invites Us to Give Thanks

Back in the day, Crosby, Stills, Nash, and Young released a song titled "Carry On." Its refrain tells us to "carry on" because "love is coming to us all."I thought of this song at Mass one day during Advent. The pastor was delivering a splendid homily about the Gospels' call for us to remain awake because the day of the Lord will come like a thief in the night. He related a story about a friend whose home was broken into and how the friend's reaction was twofold. First came the *if onlys*—if only we had locked the back door, if only I had not left my purse out in the open, and so on. Second, however, came the *thank Gods*: thank God no one was hurt, thank God nothing more was stolen, and so on.

The priest's point was that such an attitude of gratitude enables us to carry on in the midst of challenges that otherwise may threaten to rob us of all hope. He concluded by pausing and then proclaiming in a dramatic and exuberant voice: "Love is coming!" At that moment, I fully expected the church organist to break into a rendition of "Carry On." That didn't happen, of course, but I got the message nevertheless. Discipleship calls us to focus on what we are thankful for, especially knowing that more good things are coming. Such is the essence of Christian hope.

Discipleship is a call to live a life of joyful anticipation, even in the midst of obstacles, challenges, and suffering. It is a mind-set that longs for something good that we know is coming: the fullness of the kingdom of God. It is not at all like waiting at the airport or in the doctor's office, nor is it like waiting for the Chicago Cubs to win a World Series. The waiting we experience as disciples of Christ is neither fearful nor despairing. It is confident. Why? Because the kingdom we await is already within reach—in our midst—announcing that love is coming. Knowing that love is coming enables us to carry on each and every day, despite the darkness that surrounds us, with an attitude of gratitude. It also inspires us to share with others this wonderful message: Love is coming to us all!

Basket 11: Discipleship Invites Us to Live as a Person for Others

I'm sure you're familiar with the phrase *vicious circle*, which refers to circumstances in which the solution to one problem leads to a new problem (or to a new version of the old one). Those comedic greats the Three Stooges were masters at creating vicious circles. One of the most famous examples of this is when the boys pose as plumbers. Curly attempts to fix a leak in the shower by connecting a new pipe to the leaking pipe. Of course, the other end of the new pipe leaks, too—in response to which Curly continues to add more pipes until he has created a maze of pipes that trap him in the shower. Sometimes our efforts in life can feel exactly like this, especially when the "pipes" we use to "fix" things are cynicism, pessimism, and indifference.

Fortunately, one of the huge benefits of an attitude of gratitude is that it creates not a vicious circle but what my friend Fr. Paul Campbell, SJ, refers to as a "virtuous circle." When we reflect on all the things we're grateful for, we cultivate an attitude of gratitude, which in turn sparks a desire to generously serve others. And when we volunteer or serve in some way, we soon find ourselves reflecting on the experience. This reflection leads us back to gratitude and again to service—and *voila,* we have our "virtuous circle."

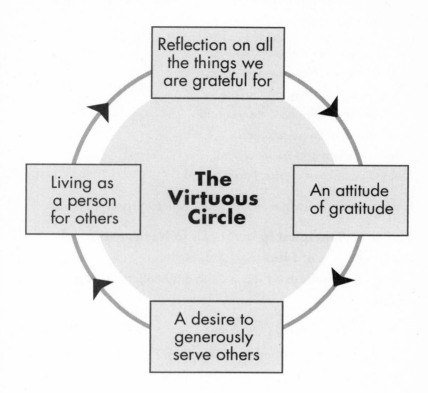

Cynicism, pessimism, and indifference are all attitudes that help create a "vicious circle" that eventually imprisons us, just like Curly's maze of pipes. A "virtuous circle," on the other hand, frees us to move beyond ourselves and to live as a person for others. And the thing that carries us out of the first and into the second is discipleship.

Discipleship realizes that there can be no authentic expression of faith unless it includes concerns for justice and human dignity. Jesus summed up his thinking on this matter when he said, "No one has greater love than this, to lay down one's life for one's friends"

(John 15:13). St. Ignatius expressed a similar desire to be a man for others in one of his most famous prayers:

> Lord, teach me to be generous.
> Teach me to serve you as you deserve;
> to give and not to count the cost,
> to fight and not to heed the wounds,
> to toil and not to seek for rest,
> to labor and not to ask for reward,
> save that of knowing that I do your will.

For Jesus and his disciples, it's all about being a person for others.

Basket 12: Discipleship Invites Us to Navigate through the Gray Areas of Life

During the months that I was writing this book, the following events occurred:

- deadly tornadoes in Oklahoma
- the Boston Marathon bombings
- underground nuclear tests by North Korea
- the Newtown massacre
- Hurricane Sandy
- the attack on the US embassy in Libya
- a shutdown of the US government

I'll stop there because I'm getting depressed. The fact is, we live in a world of great volatility. As a result, many people are hungering for stability and certainty, and as author Daniel Taylor writes, "the further away it is, the more desirable it seems." Many Christian preachers are more than happy to step in and offer absolute certainty to those living in fear. And while the gospel message should very well dispel fear from our midst, the kind of "certainty" faith offers shouldn't be achieved by checking our brains at the door.

Instead, according to St. Ignatius, faith should be based on what he calls the Principle and Foundation: "We are created to praise, glorify, and serve God, and by this means to achieve our eternal destiny." On the other hand, however, Ignatius recognized that life is filled with uncertainties, or gray areas. It would be lovely if the life of discipleship were a simple, straight line for us to follow. But as author Tim Muldoon points out, "It is important to understand that [the spiritual journey] is not a straight, easy path toward enlightenment, but rather a struggle that involves highs and lows." In a similar vein, Ignatius taught that discipleship requires us to pay close attention to our head *and* heart, or what he calls "discernment of spirits." Discipleship is an "eyes wide open" experience of the best variety.

Jesus is forthright in telling us that discipleship will not be easy and that life is not simply black and white. "Enter through the narrow gate;" he said, "for the gate is wide and the road is easy that leads to destruction, and there are many who take it. For the gate is narrow and the road is hard that leads to life, and there are few who find it" (Matthew 7:13–14). Happily, however, Jesus also provides us with the help we need to navigate the gray areas of life: "The Advocate, the Holy Spirit, whom the Father will send in my name, will teach you everything, and remind you of all that I have said to you" (John 14:26). Discipleship invites us to move forward with certainty in God's purpose for us and with trust that the Holy Spirit is guiding us to make good choices in the face of life's uncertainties.

An Invitation to Love

When all is said and done, the invitation to discipleship is an invitation to fall in love with God. This invitation to love is summed up beautifully in the following words, spoken by the late Fr. Pedro

Arrupe, SJ, the former Father General of the Society of Jesus, to a group of religious sisters:

> Nothing is more practical than finding God;
> that is, than falling in love
> in a quite absolute, final way.
> What you are in love with,
> what seizes your imagination, will affect everything.
> It will decide
> what will get you out of bed in the morning,
> what you do with your evenings,
> how you spend your weekends,
> what you read, whom you know,
> what breaks your heart,
> and what amazes you with joy and gratitude.
> Fall in love, stay in love,
> and it will decide everything.

The risen Christ asks each of us, as he asked Peter, "Do you love me?" It is important to note that when Jesus asked this question of the man he called "Rock," Peter and the other apostles had just gone fishing. The excitement of the Resurrection was winding down, it seems, and Jesus' friends were slipping back into their previous ways of life. And yet it was there, in the ordinary, that they encountered the risen Christ and responded to his invitation to love. In the same way, we can find the risen Christ "lurking" in the ordinary events of our lives, waiting to ask us the question "Do you love me?"

If we answer yes, then we'll need to take the next step: determining how our love for him will show in our everyday lives. More likely than not, this step will require a few changes.

7

You Make Me Want to Be a Better Man

Coming to Grips with Our Brokenness

Go away from me, Lord, for I am a sinful man.
—Luke 5:8

In the movie *As Good As It Gets*, Melvin, a cranky, obsessive-compulsive author (played by Jack Nicholson) seems to be totally incapable of expressing a kind thought to anyone. This becomes problematic, however, when he finds himself attracted to a waitress named Carol (played by Helen Hunt) but is unable to say anything kind in her presence. Finally, he works up the courage to take her out to dinner and announces that he has a really great compliment to give her. He explains that although his "shrink" told him he needed to take medication, he really, really hates pills. However, he admits that after meeting Carol, he started taking his pills. Baffled, Carol says, "I don't quite get how that's a compliment for me." After a brief pause, Melvin explains, "You make me want to be a better man."

Often, when we encounter someone with qualities we admire, we become more aware of our own shortcomings, and, relatedly, our desire for improvement. On a superficial level, when a middle-aged guy with a beer belly sees an attractive young woman heading his way at the singles bar, he sucks in his gut. On a more profound level, when people meet someone like the Holy Father, the Dalai Lama, or the late Blessed Mother Teresa of Calcutta, they "suck in" their spiritual gut, suddenly aware of their spiritual flabbiness and a desire to be a better person.

Becoming a disciple of Jesus works the same way. When we accept Jesus' invitation to discipleship, we encounter his great mercy, which in turn makes us more aware of our own shortcomings and our desire to be a better person. We cannot help but ask for forgiveness and for the grace we need to move forward. Walking with Jesus makes us want to be better people. "Sucking in" our flabby spiritual gut, however, is not the solution: at some point we have to breathe freely. The only authentic response to encountering Jesus, therefore, is true conversion.

Unfortunately, however, the word *conversion* carries a lot of baggage and is used in very different ways. On the one hand, it can refer to a change from one religion or denomination to another—sort of like switching your political affiliation. Such a change gives a person a new external identity. It *can* be personally transformative, but isn't always. At the other extreme, the word *conversion* can refer to a dramatic event in a person's life, a sudden, earth-shattering awakening in which we hear God's voice calling us to a radical change in who we are and how we live—much like St. Paul's conversion on the road to Damascus. Such extraordinary conversions can and do happen.

For most of us, however, the potential conversion moments in our lives pass by unnoticed, simply because we haven't been trained to recognize them. We end up instead with a string of missed opportunities. As a result of our limited understanding, we often feel that we haven't experienced, are not experiencing, and will not be experiencing conversion any time soon. But in truth, conversion is always at hand. It is our ever-present ticket to God's alternate reality, the kingdom of God. All we have to do is reach out for it.

What if we redefined a "conversion moment" as any moment in which we come face-to-face with a new experience and recognize ourselves to be ill-prepared? This happens to most of us on a daily basis. And we all know from experience that we can respond in two ways. We can either hide under the bed and wait for the moment to pass or for the circumstances to conform to our desires, or we can muster some courage and respond in a brand-new way. To make it a true conversion moment, we have to go even further. We have to get out of our own minds and put on the mind of Christ. The life of discipleship is a life in which "Christ-minded" responses have become habitual.

With this in mind, let's take a closer look at the process called conversion. By breaking it down into recognizable parts, we can learn to recognize "conversion moments" when they appear in our own lives. Then we can change them from missed opportunities into encounters with grace—encounters that lead us to thrive under the influence of the risen Christ in his kingdom.

The Anatomy of a Conversion

In his own conversion, St. Paul was transformed from a murderer of Christians into a missionary for Christ. Needless to say, this conversion was more dramatic than the ones most of us experience. It does, however, provide a kind of template for how conversion occurs—an example writ large so we can't help but notice it.

When we look closely, we see that Paul's story, as described in the Acts of the Apostles, is made up of the following moments:

1. Complacency: Saul is confident that he is doing the right thing (Acts 9:1).

2. Curveball: Saul has an unexpected encounter (9:3–5).

3. Confusion: Saul experiences a disturbance that takes him "out of his mind" (9:8–9).

4. Counsel: Saul is shown how to put on the mind of Christ (9:10–20).

5. Course Correction: Saul sets forth on a new course of action (9:22).

6. Conversion: Saul is given a new identity—Paul (13:9).

And yet when we think or talk about Paul's conversion, we tend to collapse all of the above into a single "event," as if the transformation took place in a few short seconds on the side of a road. In reality, however, Paul's conversion evolved over several years' time, according to the Acts of the Apostles. Let's look at this evolution in slow motion so as to better understand each of its moments.

Complacency

We mentioned at the outset of this book that what we desire most in life is security—which seems hard to come by in an uncertain world. In order to achieve a sense of security, we create "structures" in our lives: concrete patterns of belief and behavior that guide our actions and provide us with solid ground to stand on. We also place our hopes, dreams, trust, and confidence in certain people, principles, and institutions that we believe will sustain our way of living and give us a "safety net" if needed.

This is all well and good, right? Isn't it what responsible, grown-up people do? Yes—but only to a point. If we allow ourselves to believe the "safety nets" we've put in place are *all* we need for true security, we become complacent. When we are complacent, we want nothing to interfere with our status quo. We are confident, comfortable, and wish only to continue cruising at the altitude we've reached. Indeed, periods of complacency are what many of us refer to as "good times"—times when everything is going well and we have no quarrels with God (as long as he leaves us alone). While such periods can contain moments of grace, they can also lull us into a false sense of security. They can tempt us to think that the prosperity we enjoy is the result of our own efforts. They can also lead us to erect defenses against perceived threats to our security. When this happens, we double-down on our efforts, dig in our heels, and attempt to fortify the walls of our structures, often blocking others out and making ourselves more self-absorbed.

Saul had spent his entire life building a structure fortified by the law of Israel. He was supremely confident that he was acting in the best interests of God and of the Jewish people when he stepped forward to persecute the followers of Jesus. Why? Because Jesus' message was a threat to the security of the law. Paul himself put it this way:

> I myself was convinced that I ought to do many things against the name of Jesus of Nazareth. And that is just what I did in Jerusalem; with authority received from the chief priests, I not only locked up many of the saints in prison, but I also cast my vote against them when they were being condemned to death. By punishing them often in all the synagogues I tried to force them to blaspheme; and since I was so furiously enraged at them, I pursued them even to foreign cities.

> —Acts 26:9–11

Paul's life had been going just fine—until the Christian disturbance came along. In response, Paul doubled-down. He did all he could to ensure that the way of life he valued so deeply would continue to be guarded, protected, and defended by the structure of the law, to which he was admirably faithful.

Curveball

Life has a way of throwing curveballs at us, doesn't it? In baseball, the best curveballs have the appearance of perfectly timed fastballs. But at the last second, we realize we're not getting what we expected, and an adjustment needs to be made. Life is the same way. Just when the course seems clear, something or someone comes along to shake us out of our complacency. And these things or people that come along may very well be "good."

Some of the curveballs life throws us are minor, while others can make our knees buckle. Either way, they disturb our complacency. I always think of Darth Vader sensing the presence of Obi Wan Kenobi in *Star Wars* and describing it as a "tremor in the Force." This disturbance was upsetting the complacency of the Empire. In both small ways and large, the disturbances in our own lives disrupt the complacency of our "empire." They require us to respond to new circumstances at precisely the moment we feel least equipped to do so.

What kind of disturbances, or "curveballs," am I talking about? Here are just a few:

- a change in job status
- an engagement or marriage
- becoming a parent
- a change in residence
- an addiction (your own or a loved one's)
- any form of abuse
- going away to college
- losing a loved one
- taking on a difficult project
- a challenging volunteer experience
- a vacation
- a lack of rest, sleep, or recreation
- an increase in responsibilities
- becoming an empty nester

- a change in health (such as injury or illness)
- a change in your financial situation
- retirement (your own or your spouse's)
- a loved one being sent to war
- a grown child leaving home
- an aging parent
- a major change in diet
- facing a conflict
- legal troubles
- a major achievement
- the blending of families
- reaching a milestone
- visiting a place of great natural beauty
- a divorce or the end of a relationship
- an experience of failure
- a near-death experience
- chronic pain
- moments of intense joy
- a loved one announces he or she is gay
- receiving a reprimand

Some of these events are downright tragic. Others are challenging and disconcerting. Still others seem, on the surface, to be quite pedestrian. And finally, others are downright agreeable (for example, a vacation). Yet they all share one thing in common: they can throw us for a loop and leave us with what I call the "Ralph Kramden Spiritual Syndrome"—a state in which our soul can say nothing more than what the famous Jackie Gleason character stammers when under pressure: "homina, homina, homina." We find ourselves unable to move forward because we haven't been down this particular road before and we're not sure where it leads or whether we want to go there.

What's important to recognize, however, is the spiritual impact such events are having on us. It's a lot like Newton's third law of physics, which states that "for every action there is an equal and opposite reaction." For Christian purposes, however, we might say that for every action or experience on the physical plane, there is an equal and *concurrent* reaction on the spiritual plane. The kingdom of God is where those two planes intersect and overlap; therefore, the more attention we pay to the interaction, the deeper our awareness of living in the kingdom.

Paul encountered one of these curveballs on the road to Damascus. What exactly happened to him, we can't be sure, since his own accounts of the event (Acts 22:6–21; 26:12–18; 1 Corinthians 15:3–8; Galatians 1:11–17) do not match Luke's description of it in Acts chapter 9. What we do know, however, was that Paul experienced something that made him stop dead in his tracks and reassess his strategy. When all was said and done, Paul was convinced that this "something" was an encounter with the risen Christ that caused his spiritual knees to buckle under him like a batter being fooled by a sharp-breaking curveball.

> Now as he was going along and approaching Damascus, suddenly a light from heaven flashed around him. He fell to the ground and heard a voice saying to him, "Saul, Saul, why do you persecute me?" He asked, "Who are you, Lord?" The reply came, "I am Jesus, whom you are persecuting."
>
> —Acts 9:3–5

That which he had previously accepted as the right course of action was now being called into question. The most difficult thing about the curveball experience is that it tells us a detour is coming but does not immediately provide us with an alternate route.

Confusion

Thus begins the most frustrating part of the conversion process—the part where we feel like it's time to get dressed for an important event but our favorite outfit no longer fits and the stores are all closed. Or where we feel like George Bailey in *It's a Wonderful Life*, who concludes that all he got in answer to a prayer was a busted lip. Nothing we do seems to work. We are confused about which way to turn. We may feel frustrated, angry, unsure of ourselves, or even depressed.

For the people of Israel, this phase of the process lasted forty years and took place in a desert! When you realize Egypt and the Promised Land are about the same distance apart as Chicago and Cincinnati, you have to wonder why the Israelites covered only about six miles per year. They were clearly a people confused. As joyful as they were to be free, they were baffled about their future. They even talked of returning to their oppressors (see Exodus 14:12), a syndrome sometimes observed in battered women. Fear of the unknown often outweighs the fear of a known evil.

Paul didn't turn around and go back where he came from; nor did he continue blithely on his way. Instead, his confusion is symbolized by blindness:

> Saul got up from the ground, and though his eyes were open, he could see nothing; so they led him by the hand and brought him into Damascus. For three days he was without sight, and neither ate nor drank.
>
> —Acts 9:8–9

This period of "darkness" or confusion can be a moment of great temptation for us. The people of Israel were tempted to return to

Egypt. Paul may have been tempted to continue his mission, blindly attacking Christians at every stop. He—like many of us at similar junctures—may have looked for a quick fix or a way to anesthetize himself. But he didn't. Instead, he allowed himself to be led, gently and "by the hand."

This is why it is so important for us disciples of Christ to be present to others who are experiencing such moments of crisis: they are on the threshold of either hope or despair. It's interesting to note that the Chinese word for *crisis* is made up of two symbols, one that hints at the notion of danger and the other that hints at the notion of opportunity. Discipleship calls us to guide those in crisis—gently and "by the hand"—away from despair and through the gates of hope. This is what St. Francis of Assisi had in mind when he prayed:

Where there is hatred,
let me sow love;
where there is injury, pardon;
where there is doubt, faith;
where there is despair, hope;
where there is darkness, light;
and where there is sadness, joy.

As frustrating as it may be, a period of darkness and confusion can be a profound moment of grace. The people of Israel later yearned for their days in the desert because there, they had so intensely felt God in their midst—despite, or perhaps because of, their confusion. Likewise, it was only in his blindness that Saul experienced surrender for the first time: he had to be led down the very road he had once traveled so cavalierly.

St. John of the Cross referred to such a period as the Dark Night of the Soul—an experience of crisis that takes place on the journey toward union with God. It is during this phase of the conversion process that we are being "hollowed out" so that we can be "filled up" with the grace of new life. Much patience and support from others is required to weather the storms of this period of confusion. If we have these things, we can begin to see the crocuses of hope push through the layer of snow that has frozen our spirit.

Counsel

A counselor is someone who helps us when we are "out of our mind." When we are in the midst of the conversion process, we need someone to counsel us out of our mind and into the mind of Christ. Since the beginning of the church, Christians have realized that the journey of discipleship is best walked with another and not alone. In her book *The Interior Castle*, Saint Teresa of Ávila, the great sixteenth-century mystic, wrote,

> It is very important for us to associate with others who are walking in the right way—not only those who are where we are in the journey, but also those who have gone farther. Those who have drawn close to God have the ability to bring us closer to him, for in a sense they take us with them.

In the life of discipleship, we find our way to Jesus by walking with others and seeking their counsel. This is why, in the Rite of Christian Initiation of Adults, those preparing for baptism are provided a sponsor whose responsibility is "to show the candidates how to practice the Gospel in personal and social life." In a similar way, young people preparing for Confirmation also choose a sponsor—someone who can counsel them in the Christian life.

The counselor is not necessarily an expert or a model of perfection. Instead, the best counselor is one who has weathered his or her own spiritual challenges. A good example of this kind of companionship can be found in the Twelve-Step program of Alcoholics Anonymous, where each person in recovery is matched with a sponsor. The sponsor is not a program expert or a doctor who specializes in alcoholism. Instead, he or she is a fellow traveler—one who is abstaining from a debilitating behavior and is "working the program."

Paul, in the midst of his own "recovery," was guided by the counsel of a fellow traveler, a disciple named Ananias:

> But the Lord said to [Ananias], "Go, for [Saul] is an instrument whom I have chosen to bring my name before Gentiles and kings and before the people of Israel; I myself will show him how much he must suffer for the sake of my name." So Ananias went and entered the house. He laid his hands on Saul and said, "Brother Saul, the Lord Jesus, who appeared to you on your way here, has sent me so that you may regain your sight and be filled with the Holy Spirit."
>
> —Acts 9:15–17

The story goes on to tell us that Paul spent "several days . . . with the disciples in Damascus" (Acts 9:19), no doubt receiving additional counsel. He then went to Jerusalem to seek the counsel of the disciples there (see Acts 9:26–27), but they were afraid of him—except for Barnabas, who became a close companion of Paul's. Eventually, Paul received counsel from Peter himself (see Galatians 1:18) for a period of fifteen days.

Remarkably, all this counseling spanned a three-year period, and while Paul began preaching the gospel almost immediately, it would be over a dozen years before his first major mission trip and even longer before he penned his first epistle. That's a lot of time for percolating! Remember, too, that Paul's mission trips almost always involved companions—Barnabas, Silas, Timothy, Aquilla, Luke, Phoebe, Priscilla, or Titus, just to name a few. No doubt good counsel was sought and shared along the way.

The bottom line is, it takes time, patience, and good counsel from others to get out of your mind and into the mind of Christ. Conversion is less an "event" and more a way of life.

Course Correction

Among the many dramatic scenes in the movie *Apollo 13*, one has always struck me as particularly dramatic. It's the scene where the crew needs to make a course correction in order to re-enter the earth's atmosphere properly. If they come in too shallow, they'll bounce off the earth's atmosphere and back out into space. If they come in too steep, they'll burn up. Typically, these course corrections are done using the ship's guidance platform; however, the ship is already damaged, and the crew can't afford to use up its remaining power by turning on the guidance computer. Instead, Commander Jim Lovell (played by Tom Hanks) guides the course correction manually by keeping a view of the earth centered through his window and thus maintaining the proper altitude. After a tense thirty-nine seconds, the maneuver succeeds, and the crew's return to earth ensues.

Conversion is all about course correction. If we make halfhearted or timid changes, we may bounce in an unintended direction, but if we make changes that are too drastic, we may crash and burn. With patience and good counsel, though, we can make a successful course correction and re-enter life at the proper angle. Like the Apollo 13 crew, we need to "maintain altitude" by keeping our eye on one fixed point—the mind of Jesus Christ.

Fortunately for us, St. Ignatius came up with a foolproof technique for making a "manual" course correction each and every day. It is referred to as the Daily Examen. In his book *A Simple, Life-Changing Prayer*, Jim Manney outlines the Examen in five simple steps, all of which can be completed in fifteen to twenty minutes:

1. **Ask God for light.** I want to look at my day with God's eyes, not merely my own.
2. **Give thanks.** The day I have just lived is a gift from God. I am grateful for it.
3. **Review the day.** Guided by the Holy Spirit, I carefully look back on the day just completed.
4. **Face your shortcomings.** I face up to what is wrong, in my life and in me.
5. **Look toward the day to come.** I discern where I will need God's help tomorrow.

Conversion is not about beating ourselves up over how lousy we've been. It's about the desire to be a better person before God, in whose loving and merciful presence we stand.

If we foster this desire and stay willing to correct our course as needed, wonderful things will happen—just as they did for Paul, through Ananias.

> He laid his hands on Saul and said, "Brother Saul, the Lord Jesus, who appeared to you on your way here, has sent me so that you may regain your sight and be filled with the Holy Spirit." And immediately something like scales fell from his eyes, and his sight was restored. Then he got up and was baptized, and after taking some food, he regained his strength.
>
> —Acts 9:17–19

In the Daily Examen, we invite the Holy Spirit to remove the scales from our eyes, too, so that we can keep Christ in our line of vision, correct our course as needed, and persist in our journey toward the kingdom of God.

Conversion

It was the best of times. Like any proud papa, I wanted the whole world to know when my son, Michael Joseph, was born. I was on top of the world . . . seventh heaven . . . cloud nine! If cigars could be compared to champagne, they were "flowing freely." This was going to be great. I pictured myself singing Mike to sleep in the rocking chair as he snuggled comfortably in my arms. How cozy! In the hospital, the nurses brought Mike to us at scheduled times for feeding. After an hour or two of cuddling, he was whisked away again as Mommy and Daddy patted ourselves on the back for collaborating on such a remarkable creation. This was going to be so easy for me because I was going to be such a good father!

And then we brought him home.

Suddenly, it was the worst of times. Reality set in. The nurses had disappeared. There was no more whisking away. There were no more rest breaks for Mommy and Daddy. Life with Mike would not be a sustained Hallmark moment—nor even, it seemed, an occasional one. This baby had no interest in cuddling. His only hobby was crying. It turns out that Mike had colic, which basically means that he cried incessantly for the first six weeks or so.

One memorable night, after a day of wailing that seemed to have lasted a month, my wife surrendered to fatigue and went to bed, leaving me in charge. But never fear! I was going to be up to the task. At around 11:00 p.m., when Mike started crying, I was prepared. No sweat. I fed him. He cried. No reason to panic. I burped him. He cried. It must be the diaper. I changed him and loaded on the diaper rash cream. He wailed. I rocked him. I paced with him. I sang to him. I played soft music to him. It was now 3:00 a.m. Mike squealed, bawled, shrieked, and whined. So I finally did the only other thing I could do.

I wept right along with him.

It was a pitiful sight: Daddy holding his newborn son in the rocking chair, both of them crying like babies. As I sat there, defeated, I felt nothing but pity for myself. I wondered if I would ever be able to have fun again. Would I ever go out, play poker with the guys, catch a Sunday matinee? I thought to myself, *This really sucks. My life is not my own anymore!*

Then, in the darkness of that room, in an admittedly shaky state, I heard God speak to me: "So whose life is it, anyway?" No profound words of encouragement or inspiration, just a slap upside my head. God was telling me to let go of my old life and to embrace the new person I had become. It was a significant moment, and it occurred during one of the most profound conversion experiences of my life. Indeed, the old Joe was gone. A new Joe had been born the moment Mike was born. I just needed to get out of my mind and into the mind of Christ—a mind fixated not on self but on selfless love.

Letting go of our old self—getting out of our mind—is easier said than done. (This is why in most cultures, initiation rites have evolved: to get young people out of their individual minds and into the collective mind of the community.) Our natural disinclination to let go of the old self is portrayed hilariously in the episode of *Seinfeld* where George Costanza, now reluctantly engaged to Susan and dreading marriage, admits to Jerry that he's trying to maintain two separate personas: "Independent George" (spent with Jerry, Kramer, and Elaine), and "Relationship George" (spent with Susan). Most of all, he fears that if "worlds collide" and Susan begins socializing with Jerry, Kramer, and Elaine, "Relationship George" will end up killing "Independent George." He dramatically proclaims, "A George divided against itself cannot stand." And he's absolutely right. However, the solution isn't to maintain these two separate personas, but to let "Independent George" die—something he is unwilling to do. As a result, his character never grows but remains shallow and self-absorbed.

St. Paul learned the lesson that George Costanza did not. He learned that in order for his new self to be born, he needed to let his old self die. He did not try to maintain two separate personas. Instead, he reached the point where he was able to say, "I have been crucified with Christ; and it is no longer I who live, but Christ who lives in me" (Galatians 2:19–20). Conversion reaches its climax when we can truly say good-bye to a former way of living and being and embrace a new way of living and thriving under the influence of the mind of Christ.

Coming Face-to-Face with Jesus

One of the most depressing things you can do is look through a magazine filled with beautiful, perfect-looking models. Why do I say it's depressing? Because their flawless beauty makes us more keenly aware of our own imperfections. Our shape is not as flattering, our hair is not as thick, our skin is not as clear—and on and on and on.

A similar thing happens when we begin to follow Jesus, but with a key difference. The experience isn't depressing, but leads to grace. When we come face-to-face with the goodness that is Jesus Christ, we can't help but become more aware of our own sinfulness. According to G. K. Chesterton, that's what constitutes a saint: the ability to recognize that one is a sinner. This is precisely what happened to Peter when he came face-to-face with the risen Christ after having denied knowing Jesus three times before his crucifixion. Peter said to Jesus, "Go away from me, Lord, for I am a sinful man!" (Luke 5:8). Jesus, however, had no intention of leaving Peter—and he has no intention of leaving us. On the contrary, he has every intention of forgiving us and remaining with us.

Because Jesus refuses to leave us, an encounter with him shows us a way out of sinfulness. It is as if Jesus helps us declare bankruptcy, which provides us with protection, and then guides us to reorganize our lives so that we might emerge stronger. And this process happens not once, but over and over again. In our quest to follow Jesus, we encounter invitations to ever-deepening levels of commitment. At each level, we become more aware of the goodness of God and more cognizant of our own imperfection, which in turn we offer to Christ. The result is not just a change of mind but an ongoing transformation of heart—which leads to a transformation of the way we see, as is illustrated in this traditional Buddhist story:

> The Buddha was sitting on the side of the road when a handsome and trim young soldier walked by. Seeing the Buddha's size, he said, "you look like a pig." The Buddha calmly replied, "And you look like a god." The soldier was dumbfounded and asked him what he meant. The Buddha replied, "We don't really see what's outside of us. Rather, we see what's inside of us and project it. I've been sitting here thinking about God, so when I look out, that's what I see. You, on the other hand, must be contemplating other things."

That, my friends, is the essence of conversion. To put on the mind of Christ is to allow both your heart and your vision to be transformed. What follows is new life as a disciple of Christ—as a person capable of recognizing the presence of the kingdom of God. It is that new life to which we now turn our attention.

8

The Role of a Lifetime

Committing to the Kingdom

Lord, to whom can we go? You have the words of eternal life.
—John 6:68

Not too long ago, there was a TV commercial for AT&T that showed a young couple about to enjoy a romantic dinner at a restaurant. As the woman is talking, she sees her date look down toward his lap and inquires if he is actually watching a sports event on his phone. He denies it, but as she starts to accept his explanation and admits that she's a little sensitive, he blurts out, "Ooh!" followed a few seconds later by, "*Yes!*"—meeting her skeptical gaze with an innocent look each time. The commercial concludes with the claim that only this provider lets you download content three times faster. Despite this impressive speed, you can be sure that this is the last date these two will ever go on. No one seeking a genuine relationship is going to settle for divided attention.

Ultimately, this is what Jesus is asking of us: our undivided attention. In an exclusive relationship, both parties want and need to know that they are the object of their partner's attention and affection; otherwise, the relationship cannot grow. While Jesus doesn't need our attention and affection, he freely offers his and knows that *we* will benefit from reciprocating. This is why, in Scripture, God refers to himself as a "jealous God" (Exodus 20:5)—not because he envies the attention we give others, but because in a strict sense he possesses us. We truly belong to him, and he knows that a relationship cannot grow if attention is divided. It is for *our* sake that he is jealous, not his own.

This notion of exclusive attention to another is precisely what the word *worship* conveys in Hebrew: it means to "bow to." In certain cultures, people bow when they greet each other to signal that they are prepared to devote all of their attention to one another. This is why Scripture repeatedly calls us to respond to God fully rather than half-heartedly (see emphases below):

- When you search for me, you will find me; if you seek me *with all your heart* . . . (Jeremiah 29:12–13).

- Lay hold of my words *with all your heart*; keep my commands and you will live (Proverbs 4:4, NIV).

- Trust in the LORD *with all your heart*, and do not rely on your own insight (Proverbs 3:5).

- Hear, O Israel: The LORD is our God, the LORD alone. You shall love the LORD your God *with all your heart*, and with all your soul, and with all your might (Deuteronomy 6:4–5).

- So now, O Israel, what does the LORD your God require of you? Only to fear the LORD your God, to walk in all his ways, to love him, to serve the LORD your God *with all your heart* and with all your soul . . . (Deuteronomy 10:12).

- You shall love the Lord your God *with all your heart*, and with all your soul, and with all your mind (Matthew 22:37).

- Whatever you do, work at it *with all your heart*, as working for the Lord, not for human masters. . . . It is the Lord Christ you are serving (Colossians 3:23–24, NIV).

This is the kind of response Jesus invites us to offer when he calls us to follow him. It is the kind of wholehearted response looked for in his disciples after many halfhearted followers deserted him: "Do you also wish to go away?" (John 6:67). Peter did not disappoint when he blurted out, "Lord, to whom can we go? You have the words of eternal life" (John 6:68). Peter was declaring his readiness to follow Jesus with his whole heart—something he would become fully able to do with the help of the Holy Spirit on Pentecost, when he and the other apostles left the upper room and wholeheartedly proclaimed those "words of eternal life" to the world. Indeed, their hearts were so full and so whole that many onlookers believed they were drunk. And, of course, they were—but not on alcohol. They were "juiced," "pumped," "psyched," "cranked," and "charged" with Christ. In other words, they were motivated!

No More Carrot and Stick

Over the years, the long-running TV show *Saturday Night Live* has provided two classic examples of motivational speakers, one representing the proverbial "carrot," or reward, and the other the "stick," or punishment. The first of these speakers was Stuart Smalley, played by Al Franken (the later US senator from Minnesota). Stuart's approach was always to offer rewards through constant affirmation: "You're good enough. You're smart enough. And doggone it, people like you!" On the other extreme was Matt Foley, played by the late Chris Farley. This speaker would shout threats into the faces of his audience members, telling them that they would amount to "jack squat" and would one day find themselves "living in a van down by the river!"

As ridiculous as these two extremes seem, reward and punishment continue to be regarded as the most effective means for motivating higher performance at work, home, and school. In fact, studies show that when a task is simple and mechanical—when it requires little thought—and has a clear solution or destination, external motivations such as reward and punishment are indeed effective, especially in the short run, because they narrow our focus and concentrate the mind. At the same time, however, studies also show that reward and punishment actually have a detrimental effect over the long run on tasks that are more complex, do not have a simple set of rules, and do not have a simple solution.

Unfortunately, the church has often been guilty of motivating people to give their undivided attention to the kingdom of God through the carrot and stick approach—reward and punishment. On the reward side, we find the historic abuse of indulgences by the church as well as the peddling of prosperity by some modern-day preachers. These movements promise that if you take actions X, Y, and Z, great things will come to you in either this life or the next. Such promises only reinforce the ego and its desire to shore up whatever security it can in an uncertain world. On the punishment side, we find the "hellfire and brimstone" preachers who emphasize the threat of eternal damnation in order to encourage repentance. I'm thinking of Jonathan Edwards' "Sinners in the Hands of an Angry God" sermon, Pat Robertson's warnings that God will destroy the United States of America over the proliferation of same-sex marriage, and the filmstrips we were shown in religion class when I was a kid. These films threatened us young children with the eternal fires of hell if we broke any of the Ten Commandments! This approach utilizes fear rather than love as a motivator—an approach utterly foreign to God himself.

A more fundamental problem with both the reward *and* punishment approaches is that external motivators work well only when a task is simple, mechanical, requires little thought, and has a clear solution. Devoting one's undivided attention to God does not qualify as a simple, mechanical, or clear task, which is why Jesus did not rely on external motivators to persuade people to follow him but rather appealed to their intrinsic desire for autonomy, mastery, and purpose—which can be summed up in the word *single-hearted*, a trait that Jesus, in the Beatitudes, proclaims blessed (see Matthew 5:8). Often, this term is translated "pure of heart" or "clean of heart," neither of which, to my mind, are as powerful or accurate. To most people, to be "pure of heart" or "clean of heart" means to have purged oneself of thoughts tainted by impurity or hatred. If one is single-hearted, one is also free of impure thoughts. But one also *has* something positive, and that something is a laser focus. To be single-hearted is to give undivided attention to the one thing that matters.

The Need for Spiritual "Monotropism"

It's no secret that certain plants and flowers actually turn to face the sun. I often find myself rearranging the plants in my home so that they face the room instead of facing the window. (It's a futile effort, for reasons you can guess.) This movement toward or away from a stimulus is known as *tropism*. The related word *monotropism* is used to describe the tendency a person may have to focus on one thing, like a sunflower turning toward the sun. In its extreme, monotropism describes the behavior of people diagnosed with autism: the inability or struggle to focus on several things at once. Although severe monotropism can present challenges in our practical and interpersonal lives, Jesus is actually calling us to be monotropic in our spiritual lives.

When we are highly motivated and have a laser focus on the "one thing"—like Mary of Bethany and Curly from *City Slickers*—we experience synergy, or peace. The Catholic devotion of adoration is designed to help us accomplish this. We focus on the presence of Jesus in the Blessed Sacrament (displayed in a monstrance) in order to remind ourselves that Jesus is the "one thing," to receive his peace, and to be transformed by it. But how can we maintain such single-heartedness out in the "real world"? We can do so by shifting vantage points, just as we do during adoration. Instead of visualizing life with ourselves at the center, we visualize Jesus at the center. Instead of letting God play a role in the drama of our lives, we accept a role—indeed, the role of a lifetime—in the dramatic story that God is producing and directing.

In fact, this image of God as director and ourselves as actors is very helpful in achieving the single-heartedness that we need to thrive in the kingdom of God. As actors in God's drama, we are being called to play the role of the person God intends us to be—our true self, someone made in the image and likeness of God. We cannot do this without our director, Jesus, who knows the role better than we do. He wants nothing more than to work with us on every aspect of our performance. Like a good movie or theatre director, he points out when our performance is lacking, but only because he knows what we are capable of. Likewise, he affirms us when we get it right—when we throw ourselves into the role that was written exclusively for us and project (as motivational speaker Matthew Kelly puts it) the best version of ourselves.

Immersed in Character

It is not uncommon on movie sets to find actors and actresses who have completely immersed themselves in their characters. In fact, it is said that actor Daniel Day-Lewis, while filming the movie *Lincoln*, remained in character off-camera throughout the entire project and even asked other British cast members to mask their accents so as not to throw him off. This acting technique, known as "method acting," allows an actor to enter deeply into the thoughts and feelings of the character so that the actor can literally grow into the role. As we grow into the role that Jesus is calling us to play—the version of ourselves that God intends—we can use a similar technique to ensure that our performance is consistent, authentic, and inspiring. The following components of the technique may come in handy as we begin to "rehearse."

Concentration

Actors need something to believe in. They must convince themselves and their audience of the authenticity of their words and actions. In their book *Acting Is Believing*, authors Charles McGaw, Kenneth Stilson, and Larry D. Clark explain that, "as an actor, you must hone your ability to believe in everything that takes place on stage." In order to accomplish this, actors work at their concentration, studying their role so as to be totally immersed in character and impervious to distraction. A large part of this concentration is first identifying the character's intention (*what* the character wants to do) and motivation (*why* he or she wants to do it) and then adopting these very thoughts and attitudes; if the actor doesn't believe the character, nobody else will, either. This type of concentration and belief is what enables us to believe, for example, that Meryl Streep is Margaret Thatcher in one movie, a Polish girl named Sophie in another, and Julia Child in a third. Streep brings such single-heartedness to each of her roles that she virtually becomes the character.

In our quest to follow Jesus and to fulfill the role of disciple, we, too, are called to practice this kind of concentration.

- First, we need to believe in the role God wants us to play—his vision of the person he hopes we will become.
- Second, we need to believe that God has a plan for this process and that the plan is doable.
- And third, we need to believe that our unique role is patterned in some mysterious way on the role Jesus himself played when he walked this earth.

To do any of this, of course, we need to believe in who Jesus is, in what he has said and done, and in his promise of unfailing love for us. We need to strengthen this belief and our level of concentration by immersing ourselves in the life of Jesus and in his teaching. And the greatest source, of course, for learning about Jesus and what he said and did are the gospels.

> **Strategy 1: Research your role.** Christians have traditionally consulted two sources to discover what and who they believe in and the intended pattern for their lives: the Gospels and the lives of the saints. Reading the Gospels is by far the most effective way of putting on the mind of Christ so that your role in God's drama follows the pattern of his life. If you haven't read one of the Gospels lately, I highly recommend that you start with the Gospel of Mark, which can be read in one sitting or in shorter segments over several days. You can follow this up by reading the Gospel passage for each day according to the liturgical calendar of the church, as well as any relevant portions of the *Catechism of the Catholic Church*. Likewise, by reading about the saints, you can find inspiration from fellow Christians who discovered the pattern for their lives in Jesus Christ and lived it out in their own unique setting.

Memory of Emotion

Have you ever walked into a home and smelled a certain food cooking and immediately associated the smell with a memory from long ago and the feelings that accompanied it? Experiences like this remind us that we have countless memories and emotions stored in our unconscious. Proficient actors draw on these memories and emotions to make a character more authentic. In his book *Acting: The First Six Lessons* Richard Boleslavsky tells a story to illustrate the power of memory of emotion. In it, a young man proposes to his love on a fine summer evening as the two are walking through a cucumber patch.

The pair stops occasionally to pick a cucumber and eat it, savoring the smell, the taste, and the freshness, as well as the happy circumstances. At the wedding, a dish of fresh cucumbers is served, but no one knows why the couple laughs so heartily when they see it. Over the course of the years, the couple experiences the struggles every couple faces and occasionally they quarrel. Without fail, however, peace is made when one of them to places a dish of cucumbers on the table. The memory of the feelings of love and excitement they experienced on that long-ago summer day come rushing into the present to transform the moment. This ability to draw from the past in order to transform the present is a skill that Boleslavsky insists every actor needs.

In the same way, following Jesus draws us into a community of believers who seek to be transformed in the present by drawing on their collective memory as the people of God. Just as a cucumber can wordlessly bring the newness of a couple's love out of the past and into the present, and in so doing transform the moment, so do the words and gestures of liturgy make Jesus' suffering, death, and resurrection present to us now so that we might be transformed by them. This is the mystery of our faith. Through the regular sacramental reenactment of Jesus' life, we transform the totality of our lives into scenes of God's larger drama.

Strategy 2: Seek mystery. In order for the great story of Jesus Christ to penetrate not only your head but also your heart, you will need to experience the story through the mysterious language of liturgy. Catholics learn how to more deeply enter their role as disciples of Christ by entering into the mystery of the liturgy and the sacraments. I recommend that you experience liturgy—Sunday Mass—regularly, not just out of a sense of moral obligation but as an exercise in honing the role to which the Divine Director has cast you. In doing so, you will come to recognize the pattern of your life within the context of the story of salvation history. Pay special attention to the signs, symbols, and nonverbal elements of the liturgy: water, fire, bread, wine, processing, signing, bowing, kneeling, and most profoundly, receiving Christ himself in the great sign of the Eucharist. Become a student of the language of mystery and learn to recognize how God reveals his presence to us each and every day through the sacramentality of his amazing creation. Before long, you will recognize that you are not going through life as an actor wandering aimlessly on an unlit stage without a script, but as a key player in the Greatest Story Ever Told.

Externalization or Dramatic Action

It's one thing for an actor to internalize the thoughts, feelings, and dreams of the character he or she is playing. It's quite another to externalize them convincingly. Externalization is the process of effectively expressing, through both words and actions, the deep personality of a character—and it is, of course, the essential component of great acting. One of my wife's favorite movies of all time is *The Way We Were* with Barbara Streisand (Katie) and Robert Redford (Hubbell). Talk about chemistry! The scene that makes my wife cry every time is near the end of the film, when Katie reaches out one last time and gently brushes the hair out of Hubbell's eyes. This dramatic action externally expresses the inner reality of their relationship after all the conflicts and challenges they have experienced. Drama, in fact, is defined by conflict—two forces at odds with each other. And the only way conflict can be resolved is through the external actions of the characters.

Discipleship with Jesus is not without drama, namely because it does not resolve all the conflicts in our lives. What it does do, however, is provide us with a pattern of the life that Jesus lived so that we might integrate his virtues into our own character and respond to conflict in a corresponding way. Ultimately, discipleship, like acting, is outwardly focused. Jesus said, "Not everyone who says to me,

'Lord, Lord,' will enter the kingdom of heaven, but only the one who does the will of my Father in heaven" (Matthew 7:21). Discipleship is judged by the quality of our interactions with others, which is why John teaches us that anyone who says they love God but hates their neighbor is a liar (see 1 John 4:20). We have not been cast in a one-man or one-woman play. Rather, we are members of an extremely large, diverse, and complex cast. True, not all the cast members play their role well or pay attention to the Divine Director. But this doesn't excuse us from acting our own part to the best of our ability. In fact, it requires that we interact with those very cast members with compassion—just as the director does.

> **Strategy 3: Strive for quality interactions.** In the twenty-fifth chapter of Matthew, Jesus states very clearly that the quality of our discipleship will be judged by the quality of our interactions with others: "The king will say to those at his right hand, 'Come, you that are blessed by my Father, inherit the kingdom prepared for you from the foundation of the world; for I was hungry and you gave me food, I was thirsty and you gave me something to drink . . .'" (25:34–35). Accordingly, seek to make each interaction in your day something that you would not be ashamed for Jesus to see, but that would please him. Take it one interaction at a time and improvise, like actors are often required to do, while drawing on the patterns you are learning from the life of Jesus. Then, at the end of each day, review your performance with the Divine Director seated next to you, lovingly pointing out when your actions carried you closer to the role he envisions for you or carried you further from it.

Characterization

It is the job of an actor to bring a character to life—which means more than imitating a voice or putting on a costume. Instead, the actor must play his or her character with truth and must embody the very soul and spirit of the character. This is why many actors talk about "channeling" a character and why directors advise actors to know their characters as well as they know themselves. When actor Morgan Freeman was cast in the role of Nelson Mandela for the movie *Invictus*, Freeman took advantage of the opportunity to spend time with the legendary leader and former president of South Africa. As a result, film critic Bill Keller calls Freeman's performance "less an impersonation and more an incarnation." Interestingly enough, it was Mandela himself who invited Freeman to play the role. Freeman accepted, but on one condition. "I told him . . . I was going to have to have access to him," Freeman recalls. "That I would have to hold his hand and watch him up close and personal. The inner life has to come off the page."

For true discipleship, the inner life also has to come off the page; and in order for that to happen, we must have access to the Master. Luckily, those who follow Christ *do* have complete and total access to him—through prayer. When we pray, we "hold his hand and watch him up close and personal," just as Freeman did Mandela. And, like Morgan's performance, the result of this access is not an impersonation but an incarnation: Jesus takes on flesh through our own unique life and personality.

Strategy 4: Take advantage of direct access. The Divine Director is constantly trying to tell us that what must be done is doable, and that it's doable because we don't have to do it on our own: he is accessible at all times to help us. At the heart of discipleship is regular access to the Divine Director through prayer. And don't think that you have to get all formal at the sound of the word *prayer*. As I mentioned earlier, St. Ignatius taught that prayer should resemble one friend speaking to another. In the context of the present analogy, it would resemble an actor talking to a director whom he trusts to have his or her best interests in mind. Prayer can take many forms; however, the best advice is to keep it simple. Begin and end your day with prayer—short, open-ended conversations with the Divine Director about your efforts to fulfill your role according to his plan. By doing so, your entire day will take place within the framework of prayer, and you will be well on your way to accomplishing St. Paul's advice to pray "at all times" (Ephesians 6:18). Like Tevye in *Fiddler on the Roof*, you may find that your conversation with God weaves itself seamlessly into the fabric of your day.

Observation

Actors will tell you that their craft is simply an extension of everyday human interactions with others. Like good conversationalists, actors strive to pay close attention to the nuances, quirks, and foibles of other people's behavior. Actors learn to become keenly aware of how people behave, feel, speak, and think, and in doing so, they find inspiration for their performance. In essence, actors learn to put themselves in other people's shoes. This is a crucial skill to bring to the stage because the overall success of a scene depends on the actions, reactions, and interactions of the performers on stage. Acting, in short, is communal.

Discipleship is communal as well. Followers of Christ are not solo performers; we are members of a troupe. As members of that troupe, we are called to "body forth" the image and likeness of God—and not coincidentally, God is communal, too. God's very essence as Father, Son, and Holy Spirit is relational. The bond between the three Persons of the Trinity is so intimate and so communal, in fact, that God is One. When we ourselves behave relationally and become "one" with each other, we reflect the image of God.

Okay, but does it matter with whom we "relate"? Absolutely. According to Jesus, we must love our neighbor—and this doesn't just mean the cranky guy next door. As you may recall, Jesus tackled this issue in the story of the Good Samaritan (see Luke 10:25–37). Through the image of one man helping an injured member of a rival group, Jesus suggests that to be a good neighbor is to be one who shows mercy to "foreigners"—to those who are not members of our family, social group, religion, political party, nation, or tribe. And if this isn't hard enough, to show mercy isn't merely to go through polite motions. It's to show compassion, which flows from the heart. Building "mercy muscles" doesn't happen automatically. We have to build them up over time by intentionally responding to those in need, which in turn begins with observation: paying close attention to the needs of others, just as God pays attention to ours.

> **Strategy 5: Be neighborly.** Christianity is not a "me and God" experience; it is a "we and God" experience. Discipleship calls us into communal life, removing all boundaries from our notion of a "neighbor." The simplest way to practice neighborliness is to be observant of the needs of others and to respond when possible. This does not mean that all you introverts have to become extroverts, or that your works of mercy must be of "biblical" proportions. In other words, you don't have to sign up to lead multiple church groups or clothe a homeless person every day. Instead, you might show mercy by noticing that a coworker needs a little help completing a project or that your spouse seems overwhelmed by a task. These opportunities will pass us by if we let them, like the rich man who fails to notice the hungry Lazarus sitting at his gate (see Luke 16:19–31). Instead, we must open our eyes to those around us. Mercy begins with practicing observation. Most of our failures to live as disciples of Jesus are sins of omission.

Voice Projection

Stage actors learn early on that speaking more loudly does not necessarily create a more powerful voice. In her book *Can You Hear Me Now?* singer, actor, and voice coach Kate Peters explains that there are three keys to voice projection, or creating a powerful sound:

personality (being yourself); passion (being clear about your intention); and strong vocal physique (awareness and practice). In other words, creating a powerful voice, or projecting, involves more than being loud: it is the equivalent of reaching out to the people sitting in the back of the theater and creating a connection with them.

Discipleship is all about creating a connection with others—and also connecting others to the Good News that the kingdom of God is at hand. It is the responsibility of followers of Jesus to "project" with a powerful voice that springs from your authentic self, is filled with passion, and relies on the breath of the Holy Spirit to make an impact on others. Our mission, like that of the actor reaching out to the last person in the last row of the theater, is to reach out to those who have been pushed to the fringes and to make a connection with them.

Strategy 6: Go viral. Ultimately, the goal of discipleship is contagion: "infecting" others with the Good News through our words and actions. This does not mean standing on street corners and distributing Christian literature or shouting platitudes through a megaphone, but rather living life within an alternate reality that radiates fullness of life so that others will be compelled to seek the same reality for themselves. Our overall behavior and demeanor should make others want to say, like the woman in the restaurant in *When Harry Met Sally* who observed Meg Ryan's character said, "I'll have what she's having!" This is precisely what St. Peter was getting at when he advised, "Always be ready to make your defense to anyone who demands from you an accounting for the hope that is in you" (1 Peter 3:15). In other words, be prepared to tell people "what you're having."

A Dynamic Reality

You'll notice that throughout this book, I've been talking not about "church membership" but about "discipleship." Clearly, these phrases are not synonymous. Church membership is a static reality. Discipleship is a dynamic reality that is ideally strengthened and fostered by church membership. The six strategies I've identified in this chapter are what I consider the logical responses of a disciple to what are traditionally called the six tasks of faith formation, or catechesis.

The Six Tasks of Catechesis (Invitation)	Six Strategies for Discipleship (Response)
1. Promote knowledge of the faith.	Research your role.
2. Promote knowledge of the meaning of the liturgy and the sacraments.	Seek mystery.
3. Promote moral formation in Jesus Christ.	Strive for quality interactions.
4. Teach the Christian how to pray with Christ.	Take advantage of direct access.
5. Prepare the Christian to live in community and to participate actively in the life and mission of the church.	Be neighborly.
6. Promote a missionary spirit that prepares the faithful to be present as Christians in society.	Go viral.

Avoiding Ham-Fisted Discipleship

I've always liked and enjoyed William Shatner, but you have to admit that he is one of the worst actors of all time. The most gifted dramatic actors learn how to "do" drama without making it look dramatic. Shatner, on the other hand, is known for his ham-fisted, over-the-top acting. Suffice it to say, he tries too hard. I am of the belief that all too many well-intentioned Christians adopt a William Shatner-like approach to discipleship: a ham-fisted, over-the-top style of proclaiming the gospel. Somewhere along the way, it became a widely held belief that evangelizing—proclaiming the gospel—had to involve some kind of drama.

A good example of what I consider to be ham-fisted evangelism occurred while I was writing this chapter. In the early summer of 2013, daredevil Nik Wallenda crossed a thousand-foot gorge in the Grand Canyon on a tightrope 1,500 feet above the bottom of the canyon, all on live TV. Before the stunt, he and his family gathered with televangelist Joel Osteen for prayer. Then, as he crossed the wire, Wallenda continuously vocalized his faith: "Thank you, Jesus, for this beautiful view. Praise you, Jesus. Oh, I love you. Thank you, Jesus. Lord, help this cable calm down . . . Yes, Jesus. Oh, you're my savior. Yes, Jesus. Yes, Jesus . . . God, you're so good. Thank you for this opportunity, Lord . . . Lord, help me to relax, Father . . . Help me to calm down, and relax. You are my king. Help me to relax, Lord . . . Yes, Lord. Relaxed. Oh, Lord, peace."

Now, I have no doubt that Nik Wallenda is a good man and a man of deep faith and that his faith in Jesus Christ helped him to remain focused as he crossed that wire. I admire his talent and his ability to stay focused and to accomplish amazing feats—especially since I can barely keep my balance and chew gum at the same time. What I do question, however, is why this type of stunt, accompanied by the constant invocation of the name of Jesus Christ, is considered by so many Christians to be a template of sorts for evangelism. It is all the rage to attribute to Jesus Christ moments of triumph such as scoring a touchdown, hitting a home run, or winning a race—in hopes, I suppose, that others will be convinced of his great powers and come to believe. What is lacking in Christianity, however, and what is therefore needed more than ever, is an approach to evangelizing that acknowledges what

God is accomplishing within the common contours of our everyday lives.

Most of us are not going to walk tightropes across the Grand Canyon, and—let's be honest—many of us Catholics are not comfortable with the "Thank you, Jesus, praise you, Jesus" approach to evangelism that Wallenda represents. At the same time, God *is* accomplishing mighty deeds in our everyday lives, and we need to find a way to get comfortable acknowledging this. It would seem that the more contemplative aspects of Catholic Christianity will serve us well in recognizing God's mighty deeds in our everyday lives. At the same time, Catholics are typically reticent and often ill-equipped to articulate this reality to others. In the next and final chapter of this book, we will turn our attention to this very skill: the ability to speak comfortably and articulately about our undivided attention to the kingdom of God—not to self-promote, but to invite others to experience the transformation it offers.

Hi, I'm Wilford Brimley

Speaking on Behalf of the Kingdom

Go therefore and make disciples of all nations.
—Matthew 28:19

Let's play a little matching game. Match the spokespeople on the left with the brand they represent on the right.

1. Michael Jordan	a. Go Daddy
2. William Shatner	b. Jell-O
3. Jennifer Hudson	c. Priceline.com
4. Danica Patrick	d. Capitol One
5. Wilford Brimley	e. Nike Air
6. Ashton Kutcher	f. Weight Watchers
7. Bill Cosby	g. Liberty Medical
8. Jimmy Fallon	h. Nikon

Answers: 1,e; 2,c; 3,f; 4,a; 5,g; 6,h; 7,b; 8,d

In an effort to attract the attention of customers and develop positive associations with their products or services, corporations spend billions of dollars every year on celebrity spokespeople. However, according to Jonah Berger, author of *Contagious: Why Things Catch On*, this is a mistake. "By focusing so much on the messenger," he writes, "we've neglected a much more obvious driver of sharing: the message." Berger uses the example of telling a joke, explaining that, while some people are better joke-tellers than others, "some jokes are so funny that it doesn't matter who tells them. Contagious content is like that: so inherently viral that it spreads regardless of [who] is doing the talking."

Jesus knows that the content of his message—the Good News that the kingdom of God is in our midst—is so "inherently viral" that he need not rely on celebrity spokespeople to persuade others to embrace it. Rather, Jesus relies on ordinary people—like, say, you and me—to make his message go viral. St. Paul, who clearly felt he was not the most eloquent orator, explains as much in his first letter to the Corinthians:

> When I came to you, brothers and sisters, I did not come proclaiming the mystery of God to you in lofty words or wisdom. For I decided to know nothing among you except Jesus Christ, and him crucified. And I came to you in weakness and in fear and in much trembling. My speech and my proclamation were not with plausible words of wisdom, but with a demonstration of the Spirit and of power, so that your faith might not rest on human wisdom, but on the power of God.
>
> —1 Corinthians 2:1–5

What this means for you and me is that we are now called upon to spread the message of the kingdom to others. No true encounter with Christ results in anything less than participation in his mission. As we prepare to do this, it is encouraging to know that the success of Jesus' mission does not rely on our popularity, our good looks, or our extraordinary rhetorical skills: the content of the message of the kingdom is "inherently viral." All we must do is get our egos out of the way and work with the Holy Spirit to allow the viral nature of the gospel to do its thing. This is why the seventy disciples sent out by Jesus remain nameless—and shoeless and bagless, to boot.

> Carry no purse, no bag, no sandals; and greet no one on the road. Whatever house you enter, first say, "Peace to this house!" And if anyone is there who shares in peace, your peace will rest on that person; but if not, it will return to you. Remain in the same house, eating and drinking whatever they provide, for the laborer deserves to be paid. Do not move about from house to house. Whenever you enter a town and its people welcome you, eat what is set before you; cure the sick who are there, and say to them, "The kingdom of God has come near to you." But whenever you enter a town and they do not welcome you, go out into its streets and say, "Even the dust of your town that clings to our feet, we wipe off in protest against you. Yet know this: The kingdom of God has come near."
>
> —Luke 10:4–11

Likewise, the Gospels make it clear that following Jesus, while transformative at the spiritual level, does not require us to become something we are not. Rather, we are to become a more authentic version of who we are, continuing to do what we do but with a new, single-hearted focus. John the Baptist made this point when people asked him what they needed to do in order to become followers of the Messiah:

> And the crowds asked him, "What then should we do?" In reply he said to them, "Whoever has two coats must share with anyone who has none; and whoever has food must do likewise." Even tax collectors came to be baptized, and they asked him, "Teacher, what should we do?" He said to them, "Collect no more than the amount prescribed for you." Soldiers also asked him, "And we, what should

we do?" He said to them, "Do not extort money from anyone by threats or false accusation, and be satisfied with your wages."

—Luke 3:10–14

John doesn't tell people that they have to quit their jobs and travel to far-flung places in order to qualify as disciples of Christ. Rather, he told tax collectors to be good tax collectors, and he told soldiers to be good soldiers. This line of thinking is echoed by an ancient Zen proverb that says, "Before enlightenment: chop wood and carry water. After enlightenment: chop wood and carry water."

The bottom line is this. While discipleship can result in a change of vocation, most of us, postconversion, will continue doing what we did before in the same place we've always done it. And that's a good thing. Exactly where we are is where God wants us to live as a disciple of Christ. It's where he wants us to glow with the light of Christ so that others may recognize the kingdom in their midst. "Let your light shine before others," Jesus said, "so that they may see your good works and give glory to your Father in heaven" (Matthew 5:16).

With this idea in mind, let's now explore how you and I can participate in the mission of Christ as his faithful disciple without turning into a caricature like Ned Flanders, that overbearing Christian neighbor of Homer Simpson.

Changing While Remaining Who You Are

In his book *Evangelism Without Additives*, pastor and author Jim Henderson explores this question: "What if sharing your faith meant just being yourself?" Henderson agrees that pushy Christians are a problem but wonders whether the greater problem isn't that the majority of Christians simply keep their faith to themselves without ever sharing it with others.

I couldn't agree more, especially when it comes to Catholics. Ironically, this reality presents itself at a time when so many people in the world hunger for spiritual connection and for answers to their doubts and questions. Henderson points out, however, that "traditional evangelism is simply too hard for normal Christians. It's really designed for extroverts, those with the gift of evangelism, and the few who were created to be salespeople. That leaves us ordinary types out of the game." He insists that living as a disciple of Christ "is simply a matter of living a little more intentionally. It involves being yourself and focusing on others. It's based on everyday things, such as asking questions, listening, giving away your attention, and praying behind people's backs." These are strategies that can bring all of us back into the game!

Going Viral

St. Ignatius of Loyola would agree. He insisted that we can find God in all things. For Catholics, then, evangelization should simply be the act of helping others find God in the ordinariness of their lives. With this in mind, let's return to Jonah Berger's exploration of what causes some things to "go viral."

Berger identifies six principles that help all kinds of things—from beauty products to YouTube videos—go viral. Berger explains that things go viral when they make the sender look good, tap into what's on people's minds, provoke emotion, can be seen, are practical, and can be told in story form.

Let's explore each of these and see how they can help us evangelize—in other words, help the Good News go viral—without feeling phony.

1. Spreading News That Reflects Well on Us
Like many people today, I get most of my news from social media. In particular, my friend and coworker Beth seems always to have the

scoop on the latest news and sports—and very kindly posts this information on Facebook so people like me can stay constantly informed. Thanks to Beth, I end up looking good when I chat with others about current events or post information on my own "wall" or on my blog.

The truth is, we like to share information that reflects positively on us—that makes us look intelligent, cutting-edge, well-informed, and relevant. In other words, information that makes us look like "an insider." The most remarkable, noteworthy, and surprising thing about the Christian message that we can share with others is the nearness of God through Jesus Christ and the impact this has on our lives. Our role, then, is not to invite people into a brand-new place, or space, but to invite them to recognize God's remarkable nearness in the space they already occupy—namely, their ordinary, everyday life. When we live in such a way that God's nearness is made manifest through our words, deeds, and demeanor, we appear to others as though we have an "in" with God—something that everyone desires at the deepest level of their being. The mistake many Christians make is to project an image of someone who has it "all put together" or all figured out. This strategy usually backfires because it can make others feel inferior—or simply annoyed with our self-satisfaction.

What we truly need to project to others is a sense of the remarkable closeness of God. This is something we neither have a monopoly on nor have earned, but it can easily "rub off" on anyone who brushes up against us. I'm sure you can think of people in your life who exude the nearness of God—so much so that you crave time with them and yearn to "catch" their godly "virus." They seem to have an "in" with the Spirit, and by associating with them, you, too, experience the nearness of God. This is the key to becoming an evangelizer yourself: recognizing and embracing the nearness of God and allowing it to saturate your life so that you, in turn, communicate God's nearness to others.

Have you ever heard the phrase "thin places"? This term from Celtic spirituality refers to places where the "veil" between heaven and earth seems to be especially thin—places where one can more readily sense the divine. Such locations, whether grand (like Niagara Falls) or small (like a corner of your garden) seem to bring heaven and earth closer together. They make us aware of the nearness of God, and as a result, jar us out of our present state of isolation. We are called to become a "thin place" for others so that when people are in our company, they are more aware of the nearness of God and long to encounter him. Too often we lead lives that make us "thick" (in more ways than one!). We end up concealing or blocking the nearness of God with the thickness of our own ego. Evangelization begins with our own efforts to become spiritually "thin." When we do so, we make it possible for the Good News about the nearness of God through Jesus Christ to go viral.

Here are some suggestions for communicating the nearness of God to others in a natural, authentic way.

- Listen. Show sincere interest in other people and their needs.
- Tell someone who is feeling anxiety that you will pray for them.
- Give assurance to someone that all shall be well.
- Get "caught" pausing for a moment with God before starting a meal.
- Mention an insight you gleaned from an inspirational homily or book.
- Recommend an inspirational book (like this one!) to others.
- Audibly express gratitude for good things.
- Express sincere empathy for those who suffer.
- Show a tendency to put others' needs before your own.
- Project a lightness of being; not flippancy, but unflappable serenity.

- When someone acts like a jerk, make comments like, "He must be having a hard day. He might need our prayers."
- Perform small but deliberate acts of kindness, especially for strangers, that surprise and "mystify" them.
- Be a voice of optimism and encouragement in the face of duress.
- Model the ability to absorb life's blows without lashing back.
- Approach even the most mundane tasks mindfully—and show others that you are savoring the moment.

Traditional evangelism will look at the above list and ask, "Where's the beef?" or "Where's the 'born again'"? The New Evangelization, on the other hand, begins with inviting people into a "thin place"—the space of our very lives—where they will encounter the nearness of God. In such an environment, people will naturally be prompted to ask about the underlying reasons for our demeanor. When this happens, we must be ready to speak about the nearness of God in our lives and to invite that person, in Jesus' words, to "come and see." In the meantime, our words and deeds should be subtle hints that we are living in an alternate reality where God is near.

2. Tapping Into What's on People's Minds

Pope Francis made quite a stir in an interview he gave to *America* magazine in September 2013. In the interview, he stated: "We cannot insist only on issues related to abortion, gay marriage and the use of contraceptive methods. This is not possible." He went on to explain that "The teaching of the church, for that matter, is clear and I am a son of the church, but it is not necessary to talk about these issues all the time." The Holy Father was not suggesting that these issues are not important or that church teaching regarding these issues is changing. Instead, he was encouraging a proclamation of church teaching that is more balanced and that connects with what is on the minds of people in their daily lives.

When it comes to spreading the good news of the kingdom of God in our midst, we need to pay attention to triggers. In other words, we need to pay attention to what is in the forefront of people's minds. This is why St. Ignatius advised that, when spreading the Good News to others, you must "enter through *their* door but be sure to leave through *your* door." He means that the Word of God *must* have a connection to the lived experience of the listeners in order for it to go viral. St. Ignatius further equipped us to do this by preaching that God's nearness enables us to find God in all things. Too often, our attempts at spreading the Word are laced with "churchy" language and images of an "out there somewhere" God that have no connection to people's lived experience. As a result, we are attempting to make a connection using a weak link.

Here's an example. On one of my wife's visits to the retirement community where her ninety-five-year-old mother lived, the two attended Mass together in the chapel. During his homily, the priest spoke about the evils of abortion. Now, while I concur that abortion is evil, I'm not so sure this issue was on the forefront of his congregation's mind, since it consisted of several dozen people like my ninety-five-year-old mother-in-law for whom making decisions about carrying children to term is a thing of the past. As a result, his homily did not evangelize. It did nothing to connect God with the issues on their minds, which, if I were to hazard a guess, probably included chronic pain, loneliness, family relationships, loss of independence, and the like. While this priest's message was no doubt doctrinally sound and pertinent to current events in society, it was also no doubt quickly forgotten by that particular congregation since the triggers needed for that issue to remain in focus were not present in that demographic.

What does this mean for us in our everyday efforts to spread the message of the kingdom? It means that we need not (and should not) force people to enter through our door in order to encounter the nearness of God. As Jim Henderson reminds us, "People crave attention. When we pay attention to people because we want to nudge them toward Jesus, it refreshes them." In other words, our attention to others (entering through their door) "becomes the connecting bridge between them and God." Henderson goes on to say that "best of all, instead of asking them for something—their time, attention, and interest—we give them something—our time, attention and interest. We serve them a small taste of Jesus' desire to attend to them." This is why Jesus said, "Whoever gives even a cup of cold water to one of these little ones in the name of a disciple—truly I tell you, none of these will lose their reward" (Matthew 10:42). Jesus' message is simple: discipleship begins with paying attention to the needs of others. While evangelization does indeed involve spoken words, the New Evangelization is characterized first and foremost by acts of compassion and mercy—which begin with paying attention to people.

Here are some suggestions for tapping into the "triggers" of people's lives—those things in the front of their minds—and using them as a connecting bridge to the nearness of God:

- Ask people how they are doing, and then really wait for an answer.
- Listen attentively to others, and inquire about their experiences, circumstances, joys, and challenges.
- Get out of your comfort zone, and venture into the "zones" of others.
- Invite people into your "zones."

- Pay special attention to people experiencing a "disturbance" in life (as described in chapter 7) and tell them you will pray for them.

- Make a habit of seeking the counsel of others so that you become more adept at offering counsel to those who seek you out.

- Get in the habit of verbally expressing gratitude for the ordinary things in your life.

- Make a habit of offering a few brief supportive comments to friends on social media who post about challenges they're facing.

- Make a habit of "liking" posts from social media friends when they share an experience of joy.

- Get caught doing menial tasks with humility and even wonder.

- Help people to succeed at their tasks and to advance themselves in work or creative endeavors.

- Recognize, affirm, and encourage the gifts of others.

Again, traditional evangelism might scoff at the above for lacking "hardcore" tactics. In today's social climate, however, talk is cheap. In particular, the Christian church has lost much moral credibility, due in no small part to its own scandals. People are in no mood to be lectured by representatives of the church. This doesn't mean that we Christians have to shut up, but it does mean that we must first lead with our actions—our attentiveness, openness, and support—in order to establish credibility. Not only is such evangelism more effective and "sticky," but it is also more akin to the kind of evangelism Jesus himself practiced. It (thankfully) is a far cry from what Jim Henderson calls "terrorist evangelism," which relies on a confrontational "full-frontal assault" and causes so many people to run in the opposite direction.

3. Provoking Emotion

As I was writing this chapter, the United States government went into a shutdown. Almost immediately, social media lit up with emotionally charged messages on both sides of the issue. Carried by the strong emotions surrounding any political issue, the story went viral. According to Jonah Berger, emotion plays a significant role in determining whether a message goes viral. In essence, he says, "When we care, we share." His research shows that messages are more apt to go viral when they provoke emotions that are partly physiological, such as awe, excitement, amusement, anxiety, and anger. He explains that such emotions "kindle the fire, activate people, and drive them to take action." The government shutdown certainly aroused fiery emotions like these.

It's what God wants us to do, too. Realizing this, St. Ignatius encouraged his followers to "go forth and set the world on fire!" He may have had the apostles in mind: remember their behavior on the first Pentecost, when people thought they'd had too much to drink? Not only were the apostles filled with emotion, they were also proclaiming a message that provoked strong and even physiological emotions: the people were compelled to take action ("What are we to do?" they asked). Likewise, the two disciples on the road to Emmaus reflected on their encounter with the risen Christ in fiery terms: "Were not our hearts burning within us while he was talking to us on the road?" they ask (Luke 24:32). Jesus had sparked emotions in them that launched them into action. Indeed, they made a complete 180 and returned to Jerusalem, the very city from which they had been fleeing.

Tapping into emotions can easily go awry, however—especially when it deliberately provokes emotional extremes. Consider the "positive" evangelical tactic known as love-bombing, for example, or the "negative" tactic of wielding huge graphic images of aborted fetuses at protests. Both tactics provoke strong emotions, but not the intended one: a love of God. The New Evangelization, on the other hand, is fueled by the "sober intoxication" that the apostles exemplified on Pentecost: emotion that was unexpected and surprising, but also compelling and inviting rather than off-putting.

Faith in the nearness of God must be manifested in a visible, observable transformation of the heart—which is by nature emotional. Evangelism that is purely information-based is doomed to fail unless it can also tap into the emotions that stir people into action. While apologetics (the ability to articulate clear information about the faith) is important, it must not be divorced from emotion. Ironically enough, a group that understood this concept was the Communist Party of the mid-twentieth century. In his book *Dedication and Leadership*, Douglas Hyde—who left the Communist Party in 1948 and became a Catholic—explains that Communism appeals to people's idealism, their dream of a better world. It also recognizes that in order for people to be mobilized around a cause, they need to be inspired. "Individual members of the Communist Party," Hyde writes, "are brought to believe that together they and others like them can change the world. In their lifetime." Likewise, Hyde points out that the average recruit is attracted not by information but by seeing the Party in action and by admiring what they do on behalf of people's real needs and real problems. Finally, Hyde writes, "the Party sends its new members, whenever possible, into some form of public activity before instruction begins." They seize on recruits' initial emotions of exuberance and convert those emotions into actions

With this in mind, one wonders why, as a church, we Catholics wait until people complete a lengthy RCIA process before inviting them to participate in our public ministries. After all, you don't need to be baptized to work in a food pantry. Indeed, for us to live as kingdom-dwellers and to spread the message of God's alternate and transformative reality, we need to tap into emotions and swing them immediately into action. Recall our conversation about "benignity" in chapter 5? There, we said that kindness is shown through concrete and deliberate actions that are intrinsically good. With this in mind, consider the following suggestions for spreading the gospel in our everyday lives by tapping into people's emotions and stirring them to action.

- Invite people to participate in or donate to a cause that responds to an urgent need in society.
- On social media and in conversation, express in a civil manner your indignation over an injustice in society—accompanied by an expression of your trust that God's loving justice will prevail.
- Likewise, on social media and in conversation, share stories and images that are uplifting and inspiring.
- Tap into people's idealism (especially that of young people) and invite them to get involved in an activity that works for the betterment of society.
- Be present to people at moments in their lives when they are already experiencing strong emotions (see the list of "disturbances" in chapter 7), and communicate through your presence the nearness of God.
- Without bragging, talk about your involvement in activities that work for the betterment of others.
- Respond to the real and immediate needs of people around you with acts of kindness.
- Team up with a friend or coworker to participate in an act of kindness toward others.

Jesus said, "I came to bring fire to the earth" (Luke 12:49); he did not say, "I have come to bring information." Emotions stir us into action, and one of the most effective ways of spreading the good news of the nearness of God is to let people see us in action and to invite them to join us.

4. Offering Something That Can Be Seen

Many scientific studies have tried to determine just why it is that we yawn when we see someone else yawn. It seems that yawning is contagious. One of the most compelling explanations is that the human brain is simply wired to imitate the behaviors of others. Social learning theory, proposed by Albert Bandura in 1977, asserts that imitation is the first step in social learning: one person demonstrates an action or skill, and another person mimics it. This could explain any number of human "mimicking" behaviors, such as yawning, swaying to music when others do so, or mirroring the facial expressions and body language of a person we are in conversation with. Our brains are wired to imitate. It is no coincidence that marketers place a great deal of emphasis on visual images.

When people think of their faith as a private matter, it often remains unshared. Jesus, on the other hand said: "No one after lighting a lamp puts it in a cellar, but on the lampstand so that those who enter may see the light" (Luke 11:33). The good news of the nearness of God is like a light that shines in the darkness of a world that often feels threatening and impersonal. Our role is to help others see that light so that they, in turn, will spread it to others. This requires us to convert our private thoughts into public actions.

St. Paul understood this well when he told the Philippians, "Brothers and sisters, join in imitating me, and observe those who live according to the example you have in us" (Philippians 3:17). We are not called to put on a show, but our faith does need to be observable. One of the ways we can make it so is by leaving "spiritual residue." In his book, *Snoop: What Your Stuff Says about You*, psychology professor Sam Gosling, PhD, suggests that what we have and what we do leave traces in the world—"behavioral residue" that reflects the "meat" of our everyday personality. Likewise, as people who claim the gospel as the "meat" of our everyday personality, our actions should leave residue that points to the kingdom of God.

Unable to resist another *Seinfeld* reference, I offer the following example from the episode "The Burning," in which Elaine suspects that her boyfriend, David Putty, is Christian when she borrows his car and finds Christian rock on the radio and a "Jesus fish" on his bumper. Puddy had left behind some "spiritual residue." While these traces of Puddy's religion horrified Elaine and her self-absorbed friends, not all people would have responded so negatively. In fact, those who are spiritually hungry are likely to have responded with curiosity. Here are some ways we can spark the curiosity of others with our own "spiritual residue":

- Post (on social media or in your office at work) a picture or a quote from a saint that you find inspiring.
- Keep a reminder of your faith in your workspace and be prepared to explain its significance to those who inquire.
- Leave some literature (such as a parish bulletin) lying around on your desk at work or a table at home—ideally, something that highlights an activity you are involved in that brings the nearness of God to others.
- Carry with you or wear a simple symbol of your faith: a medal, a cross, a pin, or a scapular, for example.
- Mention (without bragging) that you are fasting or abstaining from meat as a spiritual practice.
- "Check in" on Facebook when you arrive at church on Sunday.
- Share pictures on social media of yourself at events involving your faith community or visiting sacred sites.
- Mark a religious feast day or season on your calendar.

- Wish someone a happy feast day on the day devoted to his or her patron saint.

None of the above should be done to impress people. In fact, Jesus warned against performing religious acts for show. By the same token, however, there is no reason to hide every trace of our faith from the public square. If our faith is authentic, visible signs of it can powerfully affect those in our orbit. These signs may plant seeds of awareness that gestate for months or years, or they may compel immediate inquiries into our faith. The most powerful among them can even inspire imitation, especially among the young. (And the young are definitely evangelists we want on our side!)

Be forewarned, however, that spiritual residue can also open you up to ridicule. As you can guess from its title, "The Burning," Elaine relentlessly mocks Puddy in the *Seinfeld* episode I mentioned above. However, for the true disciple, such ridicule provides yet another opportunity to model the love of Christ in the world. As Jesus said, "Blessed are you when people revile you and persecute you and utter all kinds of evil against you falsely on my account. Rejoice and be glad, for your reward is great in heaven, for in the same way they persecuted the prophets who were before you" (Matthew 5:11–12). In other words, blessed are you who can model the ability to absorb life's blows without lashing back.

5. Offering Something Practical

My wife and I love window-shopping at those "As Seen on TV" stores that pop up at the malls. They make available the cleverest products, including the PedEgg (a pedicure "must"), the Lint Lizard (an attachment for your vacuum to clean lint out of your dryer), and the Sticky Buddy (a lint roller that has "the power of glue without the goo!"). I feel like saying, "But wait, there's more!"—however I'll refrain. You get the idea. What's so attractive about these products, aside from their low prices, is their practicality, which makes many of us ask, "Why didn't I think of that?" They seem like such simple ideas!

As we set out to share the good news of Jesus with others, we need to keep it simple. The language of the New Evangelization should be direct, accessible, and practical. In speaking to bishops in Brazil at World Youth Day in 2013, Pope Francis said, "At times we lose people because they don't understand what we are saying because we have forgotten the language of simplicity and import an intellectualism foreign to our people." He added that, "Without the grammar of simplicity, the Church loses the very conditions which make it possible to fish for God in the deep waters of his mystery." Jim Henderson advises as much when he urges us to "practice normal talk." He explains that too many of us have "forgotten how to speak English. If we're going to connect with the people Jesus misses most, we need to practice talking normally, which means using regular English." He goes on to list a number of words and phrases common in evangelical Protestantism (including *anointed, convicted, burden,* and *covet*) that he facetiously says should be "banned." The same is true for Catholic evangelization. We have a rich vocabulary of power-packed words such as *catechesis, mystagogy, incarnate, liturgy, consubstantial, ecclesial, Trinitarian, venial,* and so on. These words are important—but *not* in evangelization, which is our first and preferably gentle attempt to bring people into an encounter with God. "Power words" need to be saved for the formation process that follows, and even then we need to unpack the language in such a way as to make it accessible.

Douglas Hyde, the former Communist, emphasizes that while Communism also has a complex vocabulary (*proletariat, bourgeoisie, totalitarian, socialism, Bolshevism, collectivism,* and so on), recruiters did not lead with that jargon but instead focused on the practical needs of the people: jobs, wages, food, voting rights, and so on. In the same way, we Christians need to spread the good news of Jesus using everyday language. Here are some suggestions for speaking about faith in practical terms:

- Develop your Catholic vocabulary but don't flaunt it. Use practical, everyday words to talk about your faith.

- Express how your faith has helped you in practical matters related to job, family, health, outlook, and so on.

- Engage people in conversation about practical matters they are dealing with (and not always "ultimate" issues) that are causing a disturbance for them. (See chapter 7.) Listen attentively and, if appropriate, inject an insight or suggestion that speaks of the nearness of God.

- Read books such as *A Well-Built Faith* and *Practice Makes Catholic* (both from Loyola Press) to find down-to-earth vocabulary for talking about complex doctrinal matters.

- Practice your "elevator speech"—the one sentence you can say in fifteen to twenty seconds that summarizes why your faith is practical to you.

- Describe how you draw on the nearness of God to get you through certain everyday situations.

- Share practical, faith-related ideas on social media (for example, "Ten Ways to Cope"-type lists)

- Visit www.Ignatianspirituality.com and www.loyolapress.com for practical, everyday suggestions for living the faith, and then share the links with others through social media.

- Follow the example of St. Thérèse of Lisieux (known as the "Little Flower"), who learned how to serve God in small, practical ways. She emphasized that it isn't great deeds that get the attention of God, but rather small, practical deeds done with great love.

6. Telling Our Story

Back in chapter 7, I felt that the most effective way to hammer home my point about conversion was to tell a story—my own "new parent" story. Stories are deceptively powerful. In primitive cultures, storytelling was the primary method of conveying essential truths—and from the beginnings of Christianity, it has served the same purpose.

Theologian and author John Shea explains that "the experience of Church occurs when Christians gather and engage in what is basically a storytelling process." Shea emphasizes that storytelling is important because our responsibility as followers of Christ is not to announce "the fact that there is a Mystery, but the fact that we are bonded to that Mystery." (Once again, this is the problem with so much of the confrontational social media chatter about religion and faith: too many Christians trying to prove that there *is* a Mystery, and not enough sharing stories of their bondedness to—or relationship with—that Mystery.) Further, Shea emphasizes that hearers of a story "move from observers to participants. They are suddenly in the story." Finally, he explains that stories are accessible, infinitely more so than heavy conceptual language.

Jesus, of course, is the consummate storyteller: his parables were a primary vehicle for proclaiming the reality of the kingdom of God. According to Shea, through stories and their accompanying images, "we *know* something of the relationship to God, but we also have '*some feel*' for what it is like to live in that relationship." The "magic" of Jesus' parables, according to theologian Pheme Perkins, is that "they disclose a religious dimension to common, human experience." All of this points to the fact that the New Evangelization, if it is to be effective, must be couched in the context of our own personal stories. People do not want to be lectured to about principles of dogma. However, they may very well want to hear a story about an everyday life experience in which God's nearness is revealed.

Your stories, however, need not and should not be so profound as to be out of the realm of believability. From time to time, for example, I encounter people who are on fire with faith in Jesus and whom I find quite compelling—until they begin telling their personal stories about apparitions of the Blessed Virgin Mary or mystical experiences of the Sacred Heart of Jesus. I am not denying that such things have and do occur in the lives of some Christians. However, such events are so extraordinary that they suggest the possibility of psychosis or a break with reality—possibilities best left unsuggested as we go about our work of evangelization.

On the other hand, sharing an experience of the calming hand of God in the midst of a stressful or traumatic event is perfectly appropriate. The very notion that God was near to you in the midst of an ordinary yet "disturbing" experience (whether positive or negative) is dramatic enough. To this end, here are some suggestions for spreading the good news of the nearness of God through stories from your own life—without suggesting that you are the reincarnation of Juan Diego or Bernadette Soubirous.

- Sit down and identify or write out (at least in bullet form) three to five stories from your own life when you experienced the nearness of God—the more practical the experience, the better. Don't stretch the truth or seek drama. Just tell a story that expresses your awareness of the nearness of God at a moment when you needed it most.

- Tell everyday stories from the lives of other followers of Christ whom you have known—ancestors, family, friends, or mentors—that reveal the nearness of God in a "disturbing" life moment.

- Practice praying the Daily Examen, as outlined in chapter 7, to become more in tune with God's nearness in your own life. Use insights gained during prayer in stories you share with others.

- Tell stories about people in your life who have made a difference and have helped you to recognize the nearness of God.

- Tell stories about the greatest struggle(s) you face currently and how you could use a "dose" of the nearness of God.

- Ask others to pray for you if you are currently experiencing a "disturbance" in your life. Such a request reminds people that they are in relationship with God and can enjoy his nearness—something they may not always be aware of.

- Make it clear that you have "before and after" stories that illustrate how your life has changed since embracing the nearness of God.

- Tell stories about where you used to look for security, peace, and happiness before finding rest in the nearness of God. (Young people especially enjoy and benefit from stories of our preconversion "failures.")

- Ask people to share their own stories and draw a conclusion about God's role in them. Remember that evangelization is not about bringing God nearer to people, but about helping people recognize God's constant nearness.

- In all your stories, avoid Christian jargon. Keep it real.

Setting the World on Fire

In 1871, the city of Chicago experienced a catastrophe that came to be known as the Great Chicago Fire. This great fire killed hundreds of people and destroyed much of the bustling city of Chicago. Despite the scope of the fire, though, nobody concluded that it must have been started by a huge spark from a giant matchstick. The size of a fire is unrelated to the size of the spark that initiates it.

Similarly, to be a follower of Christ and to live in the alternate reality known as the kingdom of God is, as St. Ignatius said, to "go forth and set the world on fire." This can happen with whatever size spark we carry. Each of us is called to share our unique spark and then to trust that the breath of the Holy Spirit will fan its flames and ignite the world. May we each be delightfully intoxicated by the Holy Spirit and let our sparks fly without inhibition so that others may come to thrive under the influence of Jesus Christ in a world on fire with the nearness of God.

Conclusion

You're imagining things.

That's not a slam. I'm simply stating the truth. From the moment you woke up this morning, you began imagining what the next few steps of your life might look like. You imagined what would taste good for breakfast. You imagined how you would look wearing a certain outfit. You imagined how your commute might be and how your meeting with a client or manager might turn out. You imagined how you might be greeted when you walk through the door at the end of the day.

Sometimes things turn out as we imagined them. Other times they do not. On a small scale, this can be no big deal. Our breakfast toast turns out burnt. The outfit we put on has a stain. The meeting doesn't go as planned. When we come home, we're not greeted with as much affection as we had hoped. We can usually deal with these things. However, there are times in our lives when things don't go as we imagined, and we are disillusioned or even devastated. The job or promotion we imagined getting does not pan out. The relationship we imagined flourishing for a lifetime ends in acrimony. The health we imagined enjoying for years to come is vaporized by a diagnosis of cancer. The world in which we imagined raising our children is poisoned by heinous crimes against humanity and the environment.

In short, our deepest yearnings are unfulfilled, and we feel alone and without hope. On a spiritual level, we certainly don't feel as though God is anywhere near our zip code. When we find ourselves in such a place, we are faced with several choices.

- We can grow jaded and cynical.
- We can lapse into despair.
- We can become vindictive.
- We can brush it off and be flippant.
- We can live in denial.
- We can deny and anesthetize ourselves to the pain.
- Or we can imagine another way.

That's what this book has been about: the "other way." It is the way that Jesus proclaims—and *is*—when he speaks of the kingdom of God. Jesus invites us to live in a reality permeated by the nearness of God, a nearness that doesn't shield us from hardship but that allows us to thrive in the midst of it. To live with a recognition of the nearness of God is to live in a completely different way—a way Jesus described as repentance: "This is the time of fulfillment. The kingdom of God is at hand. Repent, and believe in the gospel" (Mark 1:15, NAB).

So dust off your imagination and use it to see, along with St. Augustine, that "God is nearer to us than we are to ourselves!"

But be careful. Someone might think you're drunk.

Bibliography

Arrupe, Pedro. Prayer. http://www.ignatianspirituality.com/ignatian-prayer/prayers-by-st-ignatius-and-others/fall-in-love/.

Augustine, *Confessions* III, 6, 11. Garden City, NY: Image Books, 1960.

Barron, Robert. *Catholicism: A Journey to the Heart of the Faith.* New York, NY: Image Books, 2011.

———. *The Priority of Christ: Toward a Postliberal Catholicism.* Grand Rapids, MI: Brazos Press, 2007.

———. *The Strangest Way: Walking the Christian Path.* Maryknoll, NY: Orbis Books, 2002.

Berger, Jonah. *Contagious: Why Things Catch On.* New York, NY: Simon & Schuster, 2013.

Boleslavski, Richard. *Acting: The First Six Lessons,* Enhanced Edition. Brattleboro, VT: Echo Point Books & Media, 2013.

Bornstein, Robert F., and Mary A. Languirand. *Healthy Dependency: Leaning on Others Without Losing Yourself.* New York, NY: William Morrow, 2003.

Catholic Church. *Catechism of the Catholic Church*. 2nd ed. Vatican: Libreria Editrice, Vaticana, 2000.

Chesterton, G. K. *Alarms and Discursions*. London: Methuen and Company, 1924.

Cheung, Lillian, and Thich Nhat Hanh. *Savor: Mindful Eating, Mindful Life*. New York, NY: HarperOne, 2011.

Clark, Larry D., Charles McGaw, and Kenneth Stilson. *Acting Is Believing*. Independence, KY: Wadsworth Publishing, 2011.

Cacioppo, John T. and William Patrick. *Loneliness: Human Nature and the Need for Social Connection*. New York, NY: W. W. Norton, 2008.

Council of Trent. "Dogmatic Canons and Decrees," Devin-Adair Company, 1912, p. 61, Session VII, March 3, 1547, Decree on the Sacraments, On the Sacraments in General, Canon IX.

Duhigg, Charles. *The Power of Habit: Why We Do What We Do in Life and Business*. New York, NY: Random House, 2012.

Ebener, Dan R. *Servant Leadership Models for Your Parish*. New York, NY and Mahwah, NJ: Paulist Press, 2010.

Foster, Richard. *Celebration of Discipline: The Path to Spiritual Growth*. San Francisco, CA: HarperSanFrancisco, 2002.

Francis I. Morning Meditation in the Chapel of the *Domus Sanctae Marthae:* "Eternity Will Not Be Boring," 31 May 2013. *L'Osservatore Romano*, weekly ed. in English, n. 23, 5 June 2013.

Fuellenbach, John, S.V.D. *Throw Fire*. Manila: Logos Publications, Inc., 1998.

Gillette, Douglas, and Robert Moore. *King, Warrior, Magician, Lover: Rediscovering the Archetypes of the Mature Masculine.* San Francisco, CA: HarperSanFrancisco, 1990.

Gosling, Sam. *Snoop: What Your Stuff Says About You.* New York, NY: Basic Books, 2009.

Harbaugh, Jim. *A 12-Step Approach to the Spiritual Exercises of St. Ignatius.* Lanham, MD: Sheed and Ward, 1997.

Henderson, Jim. *Evangelism Without Additives: What if Sharing Your Faith Meant Just Being Yourself?* Colorado Springs, CO: WaterBrook Press, 2007.

Hyde, Douglas. *Dedication and Leadership.* South Bend, IN: University of Notre Dame Press, 1966.

John Paul II. *Mission of the Redeemer: Redemptoris Missio: Encyclical Letter of John Paul II,* 1990.

Keller, Bill. "Morgan Freeman's Long Walk to Nelson Mandela." *The Guardian,* December 31, 2009.

Keller, Gary, and Jay Papasan. *The One Thing: The Surprisingly Simple Truth Behind Extraordinary Results.* Austin, TX: Bard Press, 2013.

King Jr., Martin Luther. Speech to Students at Barrett Junior High School in Philadelphia, October 26, 1967.

King Jr., Martin Luther. "The Montgomery Story: Address at 47th Annual NAACP Convention," San Francisco, CA, June 27, 1956 (handwritten version). Print version appeared as "Alabama's Bus Boycott: What It's All About," *U.S. News and World Report,* August 3, 1956, pp. 82, 87–89. The King Papers Project, http://www.kinginstitute.info/.

Manney, Jim. *A Simple, Life-Changing Prayer: Discovering the Power of St. Ignatius of Loyola's Examen*. Chicago, IL: Loyola Press, 2011.

Muldoon, Tim. "Why Young Adults Need Ignatian Spirituality." *America*, February 26, 2001.

Paprocki, Joe. *7 Keys to Spiritual Wellness: Enriching Your Faith by Strengthening the Health of Your Soul*. Chicago, IL: Loyola Press, 2012.

Parkes, C. M. "Psychosocial Transition: Comparison between Reactions to Loss of Limb and Loss of a Spouse." *The British Journal of Psychiatry* 127(1975): 204–210.

Pearce, Matt. "Nik Wallenda Survives Tightrope Walk over Gorge near Grand Canyon." *Los Angeles Times*, June 23, 2013.

Perkins, Pheme. *Hearing the Parables of Jesus*. New York, NY and Ramsey, NJ: Paulist Press, 1981.

Peters, Kate. *Can You Hear Me Now? Harnessing the Power of Your Vocal Impact in 31 Days*. Narrative Development, 2006.

Pink, Daniel. *Drive: The Surprising Truth About What Motivates Us*. New York, NY: Riverhead Books, 2011.

Rite of Christian Initiation for Adults: Study Edition. International Commission on English in the Liturgy and Bishop's Committee on the Liturgy, National Conference of Catholic Bishops. Chicago: Liturgy Training Publications, 1998.

Ratzinger, Joseph. *Jesus of Nazareth*. New York, NY: Doubleday, 2007.

Rohr, Richard. *Letting Go: A Spirituality of Subtraction*. Cincinnati, OH: St. Anthony Messenger Press Audio, 2010.

Senior, Donald. *Jesus: A Gospel Portrait*. New York, NY, and Mahwah, NJ: Paulist Press, 1992.

Shea, John. *Stories of Faith*. Chicago: Thomas More Press, 1980.

————. *The Challenge of Jesus*. Garden City, NY: Image Books, 1975.

Taunton, Larry Alex. "Listening to Young Atheists: Lessons for a Stronger Christianity." *The Atlantic* (June 6, 2013).

Taylor, Daniel. *The Myth of Certainty: Trusting God, Asking Questions, Taking Risks*. Grand Rapids, MI: Zondervan Publishing House, 1992.

Teresa of Ávila. *The Interior Castle*. E. Allison Peers, ed. New York, NY: Random House, 1972.

Weddell, Sherry A. *Forming Intentional Disciples: The Path to Knowing and Following Jesus*. Huntington, IN: Our Sunday Visitor Publishing Division, 2012.

Wright, N. T. *How God Became King: The Forgotten Story of the Gospels*. New York, NY: HarperOne, 2012.

————. *Simply Jesus: A New Vision of Who He Was, What He Did, and Why He Matters*. New York, NY: HarperOne, 2011.

————. *Surprised by Hope: Rethinking Heaven, the Resurrection, and the Mission of the Church*. New York, NY: HarperCollins, 2009.

————. *The Challenge of Jesus: Rediscovering Who Jesus Was and Is*. Downers Grove, IL: InterVarsity Press, 1999.

Acknowledgments

The idea for this book was inspired by my wife, Jo, who asked me to recommend a good "Jesus book" to read during Lent, 2012. Nothing I recommended to her floated her boat. So I decided to write my own "Jesus book" for her and for anyone else who is seeking to encounter Christ and to hear a refreshing and simple presentation of his life-changing message without the burden of cumbersome theological language and without any attempt to "deconstruct" or "psychoanalyze" Jesus or to reveal the "historical Jesus" as so many authors have done in recent decades. This is simply the Good News for those who need to hear it again, for the first time. Thanks for asking, Jo. I hope you (and others) like it.

The structure of this book was inspired by a dozen pages in the tenth chapter of an excellent book, *Forming Intentional Disciples: The Path to Knowing and Following Jesus* (Our Sunday Visitor) by Sherry A. Weddell. In that chapter, Weddell identifies nine "acts" within the great story of salvation that comprise the *kerygma*—the initial proclamation of the gospel by early followers of Jesus that was so effective in transforming hearts and minds. I had heard the term *kerygma* numerous times in my life but had never seen it broken down into discrete steps, as Weddell has done. After reading her treatment of the concept of *kerygma*, I finally got it! I am more convinced than ever that we need to recapture the essence of the *kerygma*—its simplicity, boldness, and straightforwardness—if we hope, through the New Evangelization, to transform hearts and minds as the earliest Christians did.

Special thanks also to: Joe Durepos and Steve Connor for their ongoing support and encouragement; my brother Tom and the priests of Ephphatha House on Duck Lake for providing me with a much-needed "writer's garret" as I worked feverishly to reach my writing deadlines; Bret Nicholas for much-appreciated feedback and affirmation; Claire Colombo for thorough and thoughtful editing; and the Chicago Blackhawks for the most amazing seventeen seconds in Stanley Cup history!

Joe

July, 2013

About the Author

Joe Paprocki, DMin, is national consultant for faith formation at Loyola Press. He has 35 years of experience in ministry and has taught at many different levels. Paprocki is a popular speaker and the author of numerous books, including *Living the Mass*, *A Well-Built Faith*, and *7 Keys to Spiritual Wellness*.

Also Available by Joe Paprocki

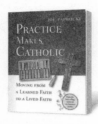

Practice Makes Catholic

$9.95 • 3322-7 • Pb

This is the perfect resource for all Catholics who want to get to the heart of what their faith is really about.

The Catechist's Toolbox

$9.95 • 2451-5 • Pb

This book of tips, techniques, and methodologies provides invaluable on-the-job training for new catechists.
Leader's Guide available!

Also in Spanish!

A Well-Built Faith

$9.95 • 2757-8 • Pb

From the Ten Commandments to the Trinity, this informative yet fun book helps Catholics know the facts about their faith. *Leader's Guide available!*

Also in Spanish!

The Bible Blueprint

$9.95 • 2898-8 • Pb

This nonthreatening introduction to God's Word uses a blueprint metaphor to help Catholics understand the basics of the Bible. *Leader's Guide available online!*

Also in Spanish!

All books are now available as eBooks.
Visit www.loyolapress.com to purchase these other formats.

To order, call 800-621-1008 or visit www.loyolapress.com/toolbox